YOUR FUTURE, YOUR CHOICE

YOUR FUTURE, YOUR CHOICE

Christian Character in a Changing Economy

Kerry J. Koller

GREENLAWN PRESS

ISBN 0-937779-27-X.
Library of Congress Catalog Card Number 93-080409.

Originally published by Servant Books as *The
Resourceful Christian*.

Unless otherwise noted, Scripture quotations are from
the *New Revised Standard Version of the Bible*, copyright
1989 by the Division of Christian Education of the
National Council of the Churches of Christ in the
USA. Used by permission. All rights reserved.

99 98 97 96 95 94   5 4 3 2 1

Printed in the United States of America.

Contents

PREFACE

Not that I am referring to being in need; for I have
learned to be content with whatever I have. I know what
it is to have little, and I know what it is to have plenty.
In any and all circumstances I have learned the secret of
being well-fed and of going hungry, of having plenty
and of being in need. I can do all things through him who
strengthens me (Ph. 4:11-13).

A friend in Minneapolis once did an economic study of
that city. He checked government statistics. He went to the local Multiple Listing Service, the Chamber of Commerce and
any other source of reliable information he could find. What
he discovered is startling.

He determined the median annual family salary for the
Minneapolis-St. Paul area. Then he calculated the costs of all
their basic needs. The costs for modest housing, transportation and food for a family of four came to $141 a month more
than their income! Remember that this figure did not include
medical expenses, clothing costs, educational fees, personal
items, life insurance premiums or money for recreation.

I double-checked his figures against data available from
the U.S. Department of Labor, Bureau of Statistics. Their figures also show that a middle-of-the-road budget for a four-
member family in the Minneapolis-St. Paul area was well
above the median salary.

Most of us don't have to read reports like this or search
government data sheets to know that something is not working right in the economy. The monthly exercise of paying the

bills and balancing the checkbook brings the reality of the situation home in a clear and compelling way.

It was precisely this experience–trying to keep up with financial obligations and responsibilities in a world of increasing costs–which provided the occasion for this book. A number of Christians whom I associate with began to meet regularly to discuss the situation and to find some ways of coming to grips with what we experienced as an increasingly bleak and difficult economic situation.

Our discussion soon went beyond questions of how to save money by shopping during sales or what to look for when buying tools. We saw that there were deeper questions that needed to be answered before we could propose worthwhile solutions to our everyday problems. It is easy to assume that the economic future will be pretty much like the recent past, but in fact this is far from certain. As we confronted that uncertainty, we saw that we needed to look at how God wanted us to live *in any case*–during economic disasters or during economic booms. We soon found ourselves well beyond immediate temporal concerns and into questions of eternal life.

I decided to write this book because little that is written on this topic considers this fundamental "in any case" question. There are many suggestions about how to respond to a possible collapse of the economy, but little about what to do if things continue as they are or if they get better. The future is hidden from us. Although provident men and women prepare for the future, it is neither provident nor prudent to plan for only one kind of future.

I will set out some principles for shaping the economic and financial aspects of your life. I will also apply these principles to the current economic situation and make some recommendations about specific courses of action to help you prepare for whatever the future holds. Nevertheless, my fundamental point is that the key to negotiating the future successfully involves not so much what you do as it does the kind of person you are. *The goal is to become a provident and resourceful person, not just to do provident and resourceful things.*

I write from an explicitly Christian point of view. However, this is not written solely for Christians, but for all men and women who are struggling to lead moral and responsible lives in the areas of economics and finances. Principles drawn from Scripture and the tradition and experience of 2,000 years of believers apply equally well to Christians and non-Christians because the principles are true. All persons will benefit from having their lives guided by true principles.

One difficulty in a book of this sort stems from the fact that our approach to money and material resources affects almost every aspect of our lives. However, my intention is not to address every aspect of life, but only one: I want to ask you how you can marshal your economic and material resources in a way that can help you develop a provident and resourceful character in the process. So, although I take our responsibility to help the poor and the disenfranchised as an essential part of Christian teaching, I do not deal with that question here. Nor do I deal with the entire area of depending upon God for our economic needs, as, for example, Mother Teresa's order and countless other heroic Christian men and women have done throughout history. The failure to mention these things in the text is not an oversight, but simply a matter of sticking to the topic under discussion, that is, how we can learn to handle the resources we do have in a better way. It is my belief that being responsible with our financial resources is essential to helping those in need. If we are not careful with what little we have, we won't have much to share with others. Furthermore, those who live by faith, counting on God day by day for all their needs, must also be good stewards of what God gives them. Learning to be provident and resourceful does not excuse us from helping the needy or depending on God. It is a way of doing both better.

One other difficulty arises from the necessity of speaking to so many different kinds of people. I have tried to write so that the wealthy, the middle class and the poor will all find help for developing their personal characters. Of course, when it comes to speaking about specific economic situations and advice, I put my sights on the average wage-earner. Neither the poor nor the wealthy will find their economic experiences mirrored here, but the principles are true for all of them, too.

Much of this book grew out of the study, research and discussion of a particular group of people within a Christian community called the People of Praise. Paul DeCelles directed the discussion, and Joe Bagiackas, Joel Kibler, Bud Rose and Clem Walters consistently added key insights. Four persons who were also part of that group made substantial contributions to the text of this work: Dan DeCelles, Patricia Lewsen Rath, Ralph Whittenburg and Jim Zwerneman. Tom Noe and Therese Cedergren McNichol oversaw the preparation of the manuscript. Although this book grew out of the work of that group, the final responsibility for its form and content rests entirely with the author.

Preface to the Revised Edition

It is now 12 years since I wrote this book. The text of this revised edition is substantially the same as the original, but much of the documentation has been updated.

After 12 years, I am even more convinced that we must become provident and resourceful people. Even though the economic situation changes endlessly, the principles to live by remain the same.

At the present, we are no longer overly concerned about the nation's supply of oil, as we were in the months when the first edition was being written. The world's oil and gas supplies are still limited, but we are not now worrying about them. We are worrying instead about a sluggish world and U.S. economy. The inflation rate is low and this is good, but salaries also remain low. The stock market is doing well; the job market is changing. We are also concerned about the rising costs of health care. The government is proposing various tax measures to reduce the federal deficit. By the time you read this book, the economic picture will have changed somewhat from the picture I see as I write, but the principles will remain the same.

In October, 1992, *Money* magazine celebrated its 20th year with a special issue reviewing the economic changes which have occurred since it began publishing. For example, the magazine highlighted some of the changes in the costs of various items in 20 years. The 1972 prices have been adjusted for inflation:

1992 price	1972 price	
$23,880	$11,824	Bennington College tuition
$1.65	$1.28	Big Mac
$7	$349	basic calculator
$1.16	$.84	gallon of gas
$9,814	$5,079	Toyota Corolla
$326	$760	New York-Los Angeles round-trip airline ticket.

Over this 20-year period, houses rose in price and fewer individuals could afford them. In 1972, the median price of a house was about $25,000 and most wage-earners could afford one. In 1992, the median price was well over $100,000 and fewer people were homeowners.

Going into debt to buy a house is usually a good idea. Going into debt by borrowing on bank cards is usually a bad idea. In 1972, the total amount in outstanding balances on bank cards was about $3.9 billion. In 1992, the outstanding balances totaled $182 billion.

A college degree is much more important in the decade of the 1990s. In 1972, the median income (1990 dollars) was $22,798 for a high-school graduate and $23,643 for a college graduate—almost the same. In 1990, the median income was $18,228 for a high-school graduate and $25,835 for a college graduate—a significant difference.

Money also reported that, in 1992, 21 percent of American children lived in poverty, up significantly from the 15 percent figure of 1972. On the other hand, in 1992, only 12 percent of people ages 65 and over lived in poverty compared with 19 percent in 1972. Contributing to these figures is the significant increase in unwed mothers. In considering births out of wedlock as a percentage of all births, the figure for 1972 was 12 percent compared with 27 percent in 1989.

In checking over periodicals to update the information in this book, I came across an interesting article entitled "How To Protect Your Financial Future" in the January 25, 1993, *Fortune*. The article summarized "Nine Steps to Safety":

Pay off credit-card debt now. Dip into your savings if necessary, lest interest payments eat your family alive.

Reserve no more than six months' income for emergencies. You could end up unemployed longer, but there are now other ways to make up lost income.

Refinance your house. By taking advantage of the big decline in interest rates [in 1993], homeowners can cut monthly payments.

Establish a home-equity line of credit. Use it only in case of disaster.

Use flexible spending accounts. You can earmark thousands of pretax dollars each year to pay child-care and medical costs.

Update your insurance. Load up on disability coverage, financial planners say, and substitute term insurance for whole life.

Automate your saving. Authorize your mutual funds to extract money each month from your checking account.

Use tax-deferred savings plans to the max—401(k)s, IRAs, Keoghs and other plans.

Invest in education—your own. A portfolio of up-to-date skills is your best guarantee of work now, and part-time income after you retire.

This list contains a lot of good advice. You will see much of the same as you read this book. Nevertheless, the focus remains the formation of a particular kind of character rather than helpful advice—although I hope you'll find that here, too.

This edition owes much, as does the first, to the work of Tom Noe. Ralph Rath also assisted in the updating and the preparation of the resource materials.

CHAPTER ONE

Ease and Uncertainty

A GREEK PHILOSOPHER who lived 3,000 years ago first commented that the only thing that didn't change was the fact of change itself. Though he lived in a world totally unlike ours, he observed changes in nature and society and in his own feelings and experiences. If he could be transported into our century he would see that his maxim is still true, but he would stand amazed. Change for us is more a fact of life than he could have ever predicted.

Imagine that he was able to revisit the earth once every century. He would probably be fairly comfortable with what he saw in every century up until around 1600. Not much would seem to have changed in the first 26 visits: travel by horse or by sail, people living in villages or small towns with a few cities here and there, families staying in their home towns for hundreds of years, people working in their homes. On his visit in 1700, he would probably sense something new happening, although it might not be very noticeable. In 1800, he would see the results of those stirrings which he sensed in 1700: industrialization on a large scale, families leaving their villages to work in a factory, travel by steam. The visit in 1900 would show even more changes: thorough mechanization of most industries, urbanization on a large scale. Even though he would have seen many changes in his last three visits, they would hardly prepare him for what he would see on his next visit in the year 2000: electric lights, computers in homes, televisions, laser weapons, antibiotics, genetic engineering, trips to the moon, satellites in space and other marvels. Yes, he was right about change. He could never have guessed how right he was.

From the time human beings first appeared upon the earth until about 100 years ago, they lived without automobiles, refrigeration, radios, dishwashers, electronic cameras, digital watches, cellular phones and the like. These items, which we count necessary to our lives, were unknown 100 years ago. Many people alive today were born into a world in which none of these things existed. By the time they were adults, these things had become necessities of life.

Yet the major changes which have shaped the modern world are not found in lists of inventions or scientific discoveries. The most significant changes are in attitudes and behavior. Many of these attitudinal and behavioral changes came about through the interplay of new inventions and everyday life. The automobile, for example, is the invention which has shaped much of life as we know it. It contributed to the decline of the pattern of neighborhood relationships, since people with cars were no longer dependent on those who lived around them for friendship. They could choose their friends, even ones across town. It also contributed to the demise of the neighborhood "mom and pop" stores, since people could travel to bigger stores with a larger selection and cheaper prices. Many other technical advances have similarly changed how we act and what we value. Many people are just now beginning to recognize the depth of these changes as they try to come to grips with handling money and material possessions.

Several key changes have had a massive effect upon us. They are relatively recent changes which we are just now beginning to experience and which many of us need help adjusting to. The most fundamental has to do with the way we are taught to approach money and goods. Society used to encourage hard work, resourcefulness, thrift and provident planning for the future. Today we are taught by society to make and spend as much as we can and to put as little as possible into work. We are taught to put our trust in the economic system as a cornucopia of goods and services. We are taught to spend our money and to extend our liability through massive use of consumer credit. We are taught to be wasteful of natural resources. We are taught that specialists and repairmen will take care of our goods, and that for us to learn the skills to care for and repair items is a waste of our precious time—time which could be spent enjoying life by watching television or buying more things to make us happy.

This change in mentality is quite recent. In fact, I can remember some things from my own childhood which highlight this change. I came from a fairly large family, five boys and four girls. It was often difficult for my father to make enough money to support a family that large. We were never what you would call poor, but my father did work very hard, at times holding two full-time jobs just to make ends meet. I can remember watching my mother do the laundry on a scrub board, then laboriously cranking the clothes through a hand wringer and hanging them outside to dry on sunny days and inside on rainy days. It was a big event when we got our first electric washer. No more wringing. No more scrub board. The saving in labor was tremendous. That washer became something of a symbol of a new way of life that we children were beginning to look forward to—a life free from drudgery, where machines would do many of the things which we found unenjoyable.

Many fathers today, faced with the difficult economic prospects which my father faced, would take another job only as a last resort. Their first choice would probably be to live on credit. Their second would be to send their wives to work and have the children cared for in day-care centers or by the schools. They would hesitate to sacrifice their free time—time for entertainment, recreation and relaxation. Times have changed. Attitudes have changed. Values have changed.

Many of these changes are for the worse. They form our character in ways which leave us open to serious temptation in the area of money and possessions. Take, for example, the difference between operating on a cash basis and operating on credit.

Cash has a very definite reality. You can see it, feel it, count it. There is a fixed amount available in the world at any particular time. In transactions, some of that money is transferred from one person to another in return for some identifiable good or service. When we deal with cash, we are forced to ask realistic questions. How much do I have? How much can I spend? How much will this item cost? Should I spend my money on this or on something else? Should I save my money rather than spend it?

Credit, on the other hand, moves toward unreality and fantasy, because there is no clear limit to what we can buy. Credit is simply a promise to pay sometime after the goods or services have been acquired. It is a matter of good intentions, not hard facts. "Of course, I intend to pay the money back. Only a criminal would intend not to pay it back." It ushers in the fantasy that we can have things that we do not, in fact, have the money to purchase. This opens new and unrealistic possibilities for us, and many of our buying decisions are based on mere desire for possessions.

Dealing in cash sets up an absolute limit beyond which you cannot go. You can't purchase what you can't pay for. We learn to keep our desires and fantasies in check. They are governed by the reality of how much we can actually spend. Credit removes these barriers and allows us to dream. This opens us to greed and other vices.

Greed is not only one of the results of consumer credit, it is also one of the causes of its widespread use and development. When you buy something on a bank card, not only do you have to pay the price of the good or service which you purchase, you also pay up to 22 percent on the unpaid balance. The bank card was not invented out of humanitarian sentiment, but so that goods or services could generate greater profits for those who extend the credit. It serves the greed of the lender. Consumer credit is successful because the consumer is greedy, too. He is unwilling to forego the purchase altogether, or even to wait until he can save the money to purchase it for its real value. He wants it so badly that he is willing to pay a premium to get it now.

Advertising is another cause of the attitudinal change.

4

Advertising has the genuine role of increasing the rational freedom of consumers by informing them of new products, of new features and refinements, of savings in cost and so on. Unfortunately, certain trends in contemporary advertising have the net effect of enslaving rather than freeing consumers. Much advertising is designed to keep our desires running high so that we find it difficult not to buy whatever the advertiser suggests.

It's easy to take advertising for granted and not think about it very much at all, unless we see something like a sexually suggestive ad. Even then, we probably don't think about the system itself. In the long run, though, the overall effect of the modern advertising system is more significant than the effect of any particular immoral ad. Advertising and other forces in our society can weaken individuals so that they become more open to suggestion, coercion and manipulation. Indeed, the future of modern society may depend upon the ability of individuals to deal with the power of modern means of coercive communication.

Surely consumer credit and advertising have improved our standard of living and some of their effects have been good. Yet Christians have clear teaching about how to approach the things of this world. There are limits. The forces of consumer credit and manipulative advertising move those limits well beyond where God has said they should be. They encourage unrealistic attitudes toward money and persuade us to adopt the ideal of a comfortable and easy life.

Some social philosophers point out that the weakening of personal character is a direct threat to the survival of our free institutions of government. From the standpoint of a Christian, it is even more dangerous. An individual who is weakened by ideals of comfort and ease will soon be an easy target for the world, the flesh and the devil. It is a matter of our salvation to guard ourselves against the powerful negative forces in our society.

A second major area of change in modern life is the weakening of the world's economic system in general and the economy of the United States in particular. The United States used to be the world's great financial power. Now Japan is the

5

principal financial power and even Japan is suffering some economic setbacks. The United States is losing manufacturing jobs to other countries. The U.S. imports much more than it exports. In the world at large, the formerly Communist nations are struggling to develop free-market economies and to improve their standard of living. Europe is struggling to become one economic force. Third World countries are trying to improve their standard of living. The world and the U.S. are facing serious challenges in an ever-changing economic scene.

The supply of oil is one problem. The U.S. now imports a large percentage of the oil it uses, mostly from the politically unstable Middle East. At any time, this import supply could be interrupted, causing at least a temporary shortage of petroleum products (several years, as U.S. production is increased) and a significant increase in the cost of gasoline. If gasoline were $5.00 a gallon, many things in my life would change. I wouldn't drive to work as I do now; I wouldn't go across town to shows and restaurants; I'd do more in my own neighborhood; my wife would shop in the neighborhood although food might be cheaper somewhere else; my children wouldn't play sports across town; we'd stay closer to home for summer vacation. The list goes on—and this is just the impact of the increase in the cost of gasoline.

Oil is not the only problem. Our system of food supply is quite efficient, supplying a large population with nutritious and tasty food at a relatively low cost. However, the price of such efficiency is vulnerability. Our food system is highly specialized. Few regions produce everything needed for a healthy diet. Most of them concentrate on one or two major crops. The rest of what they need must be shipped to them. Citrus fruits, lettuce and many vegetables are grown mainly in California, Florida and the Southwest. Apples and other fruits come from northern states. Some fresh fruit and vegetables come from Latin America and even Australia and New Zealand. This means that our food supply is entirely dependent upon the transportation industry. A truckers' strike, higher costs of fuel, etc., would have very definite effects on the availability and cost of food. Many of us would have to change our diet—we would simply be unable to pay for the kind of food we now eat. We are also highly vulnerable when it comes to the necessities of life. The problems, however, are deeper than the uncertainty of uninterrupted supplies of food and energy. The entire world economic system is experiencing a disarray which will probably not be straightened out within the next several decades. The world's monetary system presently has no commodity which supports money and its value. In fact, money, which in the past has always been a means for acquiring commodities, is itself a commodity. That is why people now talk about the money market. Money itself is bought and sold. This lack of foundation introduces tremendous instability into the entire system.

Further, the mechanisms of banking and the exchange of money need to be completely overhauled if they are to support the increased level of world trade and finance necessary for future economic growth. The current framework is hopelessly outdated. Rampant inflation in some countries, energy-caused trade-balance deficits, huge indebtedness in many Third World countries, declining productivity in some industrialized nations and other factors have caused severe damage to the world economy. We will not see global economic stability until the monetary system is restructured.

We are faced with a very dangerous situation, then. The ideals which the economic system promotes are increasingly materialistic. We are told that our happiness lies in comfort and ease, and that the acquisition of goods and services is the key to that happiness. This makes us increasingly dependent upon money and all that it can buy. Ironically, the economic system itself is less and less able to deliver what it promises. Indeed, it is increasingly unable to guarantee us what are normally called the "necessities of life." At the same time that we are told about the joys of owning a home computer system with access to libraries, entertainment and shopping channels, we find that it is more difficult to get the car fixed right the first time we take it in for repairs. Ironically, just when materialistic values are being most loudly proclaimed, we find the economic system unable to supply the very things

7

which the materialist has promised. This is dangerous, but it is also a great help. The more obvious it becomes that we cannot depend upon the economic system for the happiness we seek, the less chance there is that we will be ensnared by it. Even though, as Christians, we may resist the temptation to define life in materialistic terms, we are still affected by society's current approach to money and finances. It has already affected our personal characters and our attitudes. In preaching ease and comfort as the way to happiness, and in promising us that the economic machinery of the world would produce that happiness, it has taught us to be less thrifty, less self-reliant, less responsible.

These two major changes in American economic life— ease as the ideal and economic uncertainty as the reality— pose a significant challenge. First, how do we respond to the massive influence of consumer credit, advertising and the comfort-oriented life-style they breed? Second, what is the right approach to economic responsibility in a situation where the current economic uncertainty has undercut our confidence in the system?

CHAPTER TWO

New Men and
New Women

LIFE IN AMERICA has undergone profound changes in recent times. Our response to these changes must be to become new men and new women. Such change in us is the key to the only adequate response to the negative effect which the new economic situation has had upon our lives. We need to recapture a provident and resourceful way of life. We must change many of our attitudes, many of the values which the world's economic system has trained us to accept, and many of the ways in which we presently handle our money and our property. This change will mean restoring a way of life similar in some respects to that of our parents and grandparents. It will mean moving away from consumerism, credit and manipulation by advertising. It will mean moving toward thriftiness, prudent planning for the future, the wise use of resources, and a totally scriptural framework for managing money and possessions.

This change needs to be more than external. In fact, we need to become provident and resourceful persons. This is more important than simply doing provident and resourceful things. Although the "doing" is important to the development of the best character traits, it is not the same thing. Being provident has to do with how we view the future and how we use today's resources in the light of the future.

I know of a man who lived in a city where the top civil-service positions were filled by patronage. If you belonged to the same political party as the mayor and had worked for his election, you could count on an increase in pay and a promotion. Of course, if your party lost the next election, you could be demoted, with a resulting loss in pay. With the election of the new mayor, this fellow found himself promoted to a position which paid considerably more than he had received in the past. He had to decide how to live with this higher income. Instead of choosing to elevate his life-style to match his higher income, he decided to live as he had always lived, and bank the difference between his old and new paychecks. He realized that it would be difficult in the future to step down in style of life, so he kept his simpler, more stable way of living and built up his cash reserves. If his pay was to be cut back in the future, then he would survive it easily.

Let me describe what I mean by being provident and being resourceful. The provident person has some goals in mind and works patiently and consistently toward the attainment of those goals. He is not discouraged because it takes work and time, but he works at it until he achieves what he wants. The woman who makes it a goal to can or freeze a certain amount of each kind of vegetable and works all through the summer and autumn to do it is a good example of a provident person. She has plenty of other things to do, but she works at accomplishing her goals.

Being resourceful, on the other hand, has to do with using resources in an appropriate way. One of the most important resources of a resourceful person is himself. He learns how to do things. He acquires the kinds of skills that a person needs in order to use, form, make and repair the many things he uses in his life. A resourceful man has tools, takes care of them, knows how to use them and, in fact, does use them. If a resourceful woman has a sewing machine, she takes care of it and uses it well. A resourceful man or woman is a "jack of all trades, and a master of some."

A resourceful person seeks high-quality items, rather

than the faddish, the shoddy, the cheap. A resourceful person also repairs things rather than simply discarding them. In the interest of ease and comfort, many people would prefer to call the service rep or go out and buy a replacement, rather than repair things themselves. A resourceful person is able to maintain his home and equipment and is not totally dependent on others to repair all his goods.

The provident person usually has an emergency supply of the necessities of life, not only money but other necessities. Most Americans buy food from week to week, just enough to last until the next time they shop, with no long-term food reserve. If a truckers' strike or a major storm hit their area, they would be in sorry shape. Storing up food, money, extra clothing, fuel, replacement parts for essential tools, etc., is one mark of a provident person.

Awhile back, I received an interesting letter from a friend, which illustrates the problem:

> One summer I was fortunate enough to take a vacation with my family in and around Great Smoky Mountains National Park. We had a couple of interesting experiences, one of which was going to a spot called Cades Cove. It is in a long valley in the middle of the mountains. From 100 to 150 years ago, it was inhabited by as many as 650 people, living in very rustic, even primitive, circumstances. The buildings are fairly well preserved. We really got a sense for how these people lived. We visited rude one-room cabins, each built over a root cellar, with a very small loft. Almost everything inside is made out of local wood—hand-carved door latches, windows and furniture. The living space is very small. Many of the cabins are two or three miles apart. We saw primitive barns, mills for grinding grain, and the remains of a blacksmith's shop. Cades Cove gave me a sense of how people used to live, relying on their own skills, their ability to work with their hands, to work the earth, to survive without much outside help.
>
> Where I grew up, people could not directly provide themselves with very much at all. In the Bronx, in an apartment complex called Parkchester—12,500 apartments owned by the Metropolitan Life Insurance Com-

pany—we didn't fix anything that broke. As a matter of fact, the landlord didn't want us to. He wanted the fuses and the faucet washers replaced by the building maintenance man. I grew up in the kind of society where everyone depended immediately on the serviceman, the specialist, the supplier, to take care of even the smallest needs. I knew, as most of us in our school knew, that all those good things we were able to get to eat did in fact grow in the frozen-food department of the local grocery store. I and the children I grew up with expected to move upward economically. We were trained to think that security depended not so much on acquiring skills as on acquiring money. A whole education spiral was set in motion for me and for the kids I grew up with, oriented toward jobs that produced larger and larger incomes.

We are far less provident and resourceful than our ancestors. Extreme specialization has deprived many of us of the skills necessary to produce and maintain the services and commodities needed for our daily lives.

Often we aren't educated in provident and resourceful attitudes and skills because we don't think that they are very important. Nevertheless, they are essential to our everyday lives.

The world is changing around us, and we must change to meet the challenge. Deciding not to change is itself to decide that we will be formed by worldly attitudes and that we will place ourselves at the mercy of the world's economic system.

We need to take specific steps to protect ourselves in case the economic situation gets worse. More importantly, we need to effect a character change within ourselves. It is not simply a matter of changing some of our behavior; it is a matter of changing our personal characters.

Most of us learn as we get older that some foods which we used to devour with no ill effects now put pounds on us. I have learned the hard way that going on diets only brings temporary relief. If I return to my regular eating habits, the pounds go right back on. The only way to straighten things out is to change both the way I eat and my attitude toward food. Today we have the same kind of situation in the sphere of economics. We might take this or that action but, unless we change our consumerist mentality, we will not be able to cope successfully. We must train ourselves to resist the efforts of those forces in our society which promote a worldly mindset.

One of the first steps in making the changes I am suggesting is to take stock of your present situation. Examine your current attitudes and life-style. How are you handling your money now? Do you have a budget, or do you just spend your money on what you want at the moment you want it?

Having a budget is essential to making headway. A budget gives you control of how you spend your money, provides a record of the past, and is an important device for assessing your current economic situation. Later I will give a fuller treatment of how to budget, but at this point it is important to see how you are managing your money. A budget should list all those things which you are obliged to pay: regular support for the Lord's work, house payments or rent, food, utilities, clothing, medical expenses, transportation, etc. It is not simply a historical record of how you spend your money, but an aid in controlling expenses. In each of these categories, you should write down how much you will spend and stick to it. The tough but absolutely essential part is not to spend more in any category than you have written down. This takes discipline and self-control, but it is the only way to get mastery over your finances.

When you first use a budget, you might discover that the amount of money spent in some category is considerably more than you allocated. This means that either the original amount was inaccurate, or that you are spending more than you should. You have to make an honest reassessment of the situation. If you need more money in a category, assign it. Of course, assigning more money to one category means that it has to be taken from another. This leads to further reassessments and decisions. Do you need this more than that? Do you make enough money at your present job? Should you change jobs or take an extra job?

This kind of exercise is important not simply because it puts order into your spending, but because it forces you to take responsible action. When you have to decide about spending money for this rather than that, you are moving toward a more realistic life-style. Confronting such choices and making decisions will form valuable character traits.

Many times people make budgets with all the right intentions but don't stick to them. Often they simply forget about them and return to their earlier way of doing things. Sometimes they stick to them in some categories but then spend their remaining funds in wildly extravagant ways. A person who doesn't have enough money to pay his bills might buy something frivolous: an expensive camera, another pair of shoes or unneeded clothing. This is a temptation to be resisted. It is a matter of discipline and strength. If you feel that you do not have the strength, find a friend or member of the clergy to encourage and aid you. After you successfully resist the temptation a few times, you will gain enough strength to resist it more effectively in the future.

Another area to consider has to do with your desire for material goods. Have you been deeply influenced by advertising and the media? Have you internalized a strong desire to possess things, to have money, to live the so-called good life? These are all to be resisted. One of the best ways to do this is to put yourself out of the reach of most advertising. If television ads affect you, cut back on your viewing. If it's the newspaper, stop reading the ads except when you have to. Attitudes have a cause. If you remove the cause, you will go a long way toward removing the attitude. Often, however, this is not enough because the problem is within us. We have to repent of the desires we have, admitting that they are wrong, seeking God's forgiveness, and deciding that we will act differently in the future.

A key to meeting the challenges of our time is the recovery of a provident and resourceful style of life. However, we do not want simply to recover a specific historical way of life, we want to recover a Christian way of life. Before we proceed to discuss the details of how to live providently and resourcefully, we need to have a totally Christian framework for managing money and possessions.

CHAPTER THREE

A Scriptural Perspective

BEING A PROVIDENT AND RESOURCEFUL PERSON is one thing; being a provident and resourceful Christian is another. The provident and resourceful Christian allows all his attitudes to be formed by God's word through Scripture and church teaching. Five principles, drawn from Scripture, form the foundation of a Christian mentality about money and finances. Following these principles is essential as Christians develop their response to the challenges of today's world.

1. The present form of this world is passing away.

2. The economic systems of this world are one of God's ways to provide for his creatures.

3. God's provision has a twofold purpose: to give us enough resources to support his work and to provide for our sustenance. He calls us to put his work first.

4. We should always live in a way that prepares us for economic change.

5. As we prepare for the future, we want to take seriously the scriptural warnings about the dangers that accompany the pursuit or possession of wealth.

In this chapter we will focus on the first of these principles. The first thing to realize is that there are real dangers in focusing on financial matters. We can become so concerned about material things and earthly goods that we lose sight of the goal. We need to keep God's perspective, in order to avoid developing a wrong perspective. For this we look to Scripture. In his first letter to the Corinthians, Paul tells us that "the present form of this world is passing away" (1 Cor. 7:31).

When we deal with money, possessions, economics and the like, it is important to develop a perspective that is not limited to the usual framework of human time. The psalmist, for example, sees time as God wants us to see it.

Lord, you have been our dwelling place
    in all generations.
Before the mountains were brought forth,
    or ever you had formed the earth and the world,
    from everlasting to everlasting you are God.
You turn us back to dust,
    and say, "Turn back, you mortals."
For a thousand years in your sight are like yesterday
    when it is past,
    or like a watch in the night.
You sweep them away; they are like a dream,
    like grass that is renewed in the morning;
in the morning it flourishes and is renewed;
    in the evening it fades and withers.
For we are consumed by your anger;
    by your wrath we are overwhelmed.
You have set our iniquities before you,
    our secret sins in the light of your countenance.
For all our days pass away under your wrath,
    our years come to an end like a sigh.
The days of our life are seventy years,
    or perhaps eighty if we are strong;
even then their span is only toil and trouble;
    they are soon gone, and we fly away.
Who considers the power of your anger?
    your wrath is as great as the fear due you.
So teach us to count our days
    that we may gain a wise heart (Ps. 90:1-12).

Our perception of time changes as we progress from infancy through adolescence, into maturity and old age. Children think in terms of what is most immediate to them—the needs and events of the day, even of the minute. Tell a young child that Christmas is six months away, and he will not be able to understand the length of time involved. The next day he might ask, "Is it Christmas now?" Later in life, perhaps as a teenager, he will be able to think in terms of longer spans of time. "Next summer I'll try to get a job in the factory." "When I graduate from high school, I want to go to college." In fact, one of the signs of adulthood and maturity is the ability to think in terms of the span of one's life. At each stage of life, our awareness of time broadens. We begin to regulate our immediate needs and desires in relation to our long-term needs and desires.

I recall my father telling me, "It may seem like the days drag now, but wait till you're my age and you'll see that things will go by very quickly." As our perspective on time changes, our perspective on life changes also. As a young man, a friend of mine once attended the funeral of a man in his 60s. Most of those who attended the services were elderly people. They talked about their lives in 10- and 20-year segments. My friend, in his mid-20s at the time, felt odd as they talked about segments of their lives which were equal in span to his entire life. Their viewpoints were broader and larger than his; they had experienced more of life and their perspectives differed in many ways from his.

As we grow in age and maturity, our perspective on life changes from short-term to long-term. We begin to think differently about what we find valuable and what we find worthless. We begin to see things in light of the entire process of our lives. We realize that we won't live forever. Often, it is this realization of impending death that first prompts us to take that careful, slow, long-term look at life. "The days of our life are seventy years, or perhaps eighty if we are strong; even then their span is only toil and trouble; they are soon gone, and we fly away."

It's natural to see our lives as dust blown across the silent desert, to see death as the impassable barrier. However, we also read, "So teach us to count our days that we may gain a wise heart." Only the man with a heart of wisdom can see beyond a view of death that takes no assessment of eternity. For him, life extends into eternity, and his decisions are made in terms of this larger perspective.

Yet, in a certain sense, even the level of spiritual wisdom which allows us to see beyond our own death is incomplete. The coming of Christ has given new urgency to this ancient mystery of the passing of time. It is no longer sufficient simply to act with wisdom in view of our individual death. Rather, we must act wisely in light of an even larger perspective, one that takes into account the end of time itself. An individual's death—the end of time for each of us—is assumed under a larger happening, a part of God's plan that is rapidly coming to fulfillment: "The appointed time has grown short. . . . For the present form of this world is passing away" (1 Cor. 7:29, 31). History will come to a close at a certain point, and the spiritual man must guide his decisions so that he takes into account not only his personal death, but also the death of the universe, the climax and culmination of God's creative action.

Carl Sagan, an astronomer, developed an interesting calendar in which all history is compressed into one year. He made January 1 the time in prehistory that some scientists call the Big Bang, when all the created matter might have exploded outward from a single point. January 1 a year later is the present. Sagan then fits the major events for which scientists have evidence into this span of a year. The day on which our galaxy coalesces is around May 1. The planet earth solidifies around September. It is not until the first day of December that an atmosphere with a significant amount of oxygen begins to form. Halfway through that month our fellow creatures begin to appear. On Christmas Eve the first dinosaurs appear. On New Year's Eve, around 10:30 p.m., Adam and Eve walk the face of the earth. Four minutes before midnight, the most recent period of glaciation begins. One second before midnight, Columbus discovers America. All recorded history occupies only the final 10 seconds of the calendar year.

This image helps us to understand that God is "from everlasting to everlasting." The life of an individual, compared with the life of the universe, is like a snap of the fingers. Like a wildflower, which withers when it is cut, the life of a human being is a small thing on the scale of the whole of creation. The Lord existed before creation; he will exist after creation comes to its climax. It is simply a matter of realism for us to consider the fragility of our life on earth. Here for only a moment, we know that the major part of our life's existence will occur after our individual death, when we come into eternity.

The New Testament often suggests that our personal realization of the nearness of death and the debt which each of us must pay to death is an opportunity to form a new perspective on life. When we first confront the fact that we must die, it changes us. When God reveals to us personally – either through Scripture or through experiencing contact with death – that there is a final end to all things, his purpose is to influence our behavior. "The present form of this world is passing away" looks like a simple statement of fact. In reality it is a principle which God expects us to use to moderate our style of life.

> And he said to them, "Take care! Be on your guard against all kinds of greed, for one's life does not consist in the abundance of possessions." Then he told them a parable: "The land of a rich man produced abundantly. And he thought to himself, 'What should I do, for I have no place to store my crops?' Then he said, 'I will do this: I will pull down my barns and build larger ones, and there I will store all my grain and my goods. And I will say to my soul, 'Soul, you have ample goods laid up for many years; relax, eat, drink, be merry.' But God said to him, 'You fool! This night your life is being demanded of you. And the things you have prepared, whose will they be?' So it is with those who store up treasures for themselves, but are not rich toward God" (Lk. 12:15–21).

Our death is not a distant experience which has no bearing on daily behavior.

The wise man realizes that he is going to die and lives his

life accordingly. He is especially careful regarding the proper use of this world's treasures with respect to the needs of his fellow human beings.

> There was a rich man who was dressed in purple and fine linen and who feasted sumptuously every day. And at his gate lay a poor man named Lazarus, covered with sores, who longed to satisfy his hunger with what fell from the rich man's table; even the dogs would come and lick his sores. The poor man died and was carried away by the angels to be with Abraham. The rich man also died and was buried. In Hades, where he was being tormented, he looked up and saw Abraham far away with Lazarus by his side. He called out, "Father Abraham, have mercy on me, and send Lazarus to dip the tip of his finger in water and cool my tongue; for I am in agony in these flames." But Abraham said, "Child, remember that during your lifetime you received your good things, and Lazarus in like manner evil things; but now he is comforted here, and you are in agony. Besides all this, between you and us a great chasm has been fixed, so that those who might want to pass from here to you cannot do so, and no one can cross from there to us" (Lk. 16: 19–26).

The use of the goods of this world is regulated by the justice of God. Those who have kept for themselves an excess of this world's goods will be punished in the life to come. On the other side of death, God's standard will be invoked. Sitting in judgment, he will redress the inequities and injustices of this world.

The rich man and the poor man alike will find that whatever possessions they have acquired, whatever they own, will fail them on the night their souls are required of them. That time will come for every one of us, and no amount of possessions will gain us access to the bosom of Abraham. It may get us into a prestigious country club, but it won't get us into the only club that counts, where a lifetime membership means eternity. Indeed, for many, the pursuit of earthly treasures is an obstacle, preventing them from finding eternal treasure.

There is wisdom to be acquired from meditating on and understanding what it means that we are here only for a short time. One thing we can learn is to distinguish the means from the end. All of us have only one end ultimately, the end for which we were made. We may choose our own goals of various sorts, but we were made by someone else. We are his. We belong to him and he has an end for each of us—to live with him forever. This is our end, toward which all our efforts must be directed.

God has put other created things in our care, and we have to view these as means for attaining our end. The fellow who thought, I've got enough laid up for myself in my barns, so I'm going to eat, drink and be merry, had a very short-term perspective. He could not see much further than a few years ahead. A short-term perspective leads to an approach to life in which we focus on things—acquiring, enjoying and thinking of ways to protect our possessions. Our decisions will all be geared toward how they will enhance our material well-being and our pleasure.

A long-term perspective, however, tells us that we will be judged not by what we have possessed but by how we have used our possessions. Did we use them as a means for attaining our end? Two Scripture passages are especially helpful in seeing this.

> He said also to the one who had invited him, "When you give a luncheon or a dinner, do not invite your friends or your brothers or your relatives or rich neighbors, in case they may invite you in return, and you would be repaid. But when you give a banquet, invite the poor, the crippled, the lame, and the blind. And you will be blessed, because they cannot repay you, for you will be repaid at the resurrection of the righteous" (Lk. 14: 12–13).

> As for those who in the present age are rich, command them not to be haughty, or to set their hopes on the uncertainty of riches, but rather on God who richly provides us with everything for our enjoyment. They are to do good, to be rich in good works, generous, and ready

to share, thus storing up for themselves the treasure of a good foundation for the future, so that they may take hold of the life that really is life (1 Tm. 6:17–19).

Don't think of repayment within a short period of time, such as a year or two years, or even 50 years. Instead, use your material possessions according to God's plan, and be repaid on the long term, at the resurrection of the just. Receive now a treasure in heaven that does not fail.

CHAPTER FOUR

God Provides for All His Creatures

THE SECOND PRINCIPLE is that the economic system of the world is one of the ways in which God makes provision for all his creatures. Psalm 104 shows how the Lord has provided for all of us – the worms, the dinosaurs and mankind – in marvelous and complex ways.

> You make springs gush forth in the valleys;
>   they flow between the hills,
> giving drink to every wild animal;
>   the wild asses quench their thirst.
> By the streams the birds of the air have their habitation;
>   they sing among the branches.
> From your lofty abode you water the mountains;
>   the earth is satisfied with the fruit of your work.
> You cause the grass to grow for the cattle,
>   and plants for people to use,
> to bring forth food from the earth,
>   and wine to gladden the human heart
>   (Ps. 104:10–15).

God takes care of all his creatures, not just his own people. "Love your enemies and pray for those who persecute you, so that you may be children of your Father in heaven; for he makes his sun rise on the evil and on the good, and sends rain on the righteous and on the unrighteous" (Mt. 5:44–45). The evil have farms, and God sends his sun and rain to nourish their crops just as he does to the crops of the just.

If we look at how God has distributed the resources of this earth, the various climatological conditions and the talents of all the various peoples of the world, we see that his creation suggests a system of cooperation and trade meant to be beneficial to all. One part of the world is rich in iron ore, another in coal. Through trade, both can make steel. You can send wheat from the United States to another part of the world and come back with tin, coffee and oil. Mutual cooperation among the peoples of the earth should result in a way of distributing natural resources according to God's plan.

This cooperative effort which economic interdependence brings about is also important because it furthers God's goal of developing brotherhood in the entire human race. Cooperation brings people together in towns, villages and cities, where they begin to share their lives. It forms the basis of human culture and weaves the great tapestry of human history. In this world order, God works out all that he has in mind for mankind.

This affects Christians in two ways. First, we are involved in the world's economy because it is the way God provides for our needs. Our participation can help in the provision for all, because of our sensitivity to God's plan. God entrusts the administration of this overall distribution plan largely to human authorities, and he holds them accountable for meeting the material needs of people. The inequitable distribution of material resources is due to sin in the world, to greed and the abuse of authority. God set the world up to work right: there is enough of everything for everyone to be taken care of.

Second, we are obliged to be good citizens diligently engaged in productive work, helping the whole system to operate properly. We should also participate in the political life of our community in order to promote the good of all by influencing society toward God's purposes. We also further God's plan by ministering to the poor and by giving alms.

These are good reasons to stay involved in the world around us and its economic system, but we should not be naive about our involvement in the world. Although Jesus has overcome sin, the world is still vulnerable to the power of the devil, the evil one. When we become involved in the world we run real risks of being cheated, of being corrupted, of being persecuted.

There are, as we all know, wicked persons, rich and powerful, who will take advantage of good men and women for their own sinful gain. "Is it not the rich who oppress you? Is it not they who drag you into court? Is it not they who blaspheme the excellent name that was invoked over you?" (Jas. 2:6–7). Getting cheated out of our money would not be so terrible, except that it is actually God's money, given to us to be used for his purposes. The real crime is that God's money is stolen, diverted from his loving purposes, and used for sinful purposes.

We cannot lay all the blame at the feet of the rich, of course. We know that "all have sinned and fall short of the glory of God" (Rm. 3:23). Just as there are wicked men who are rich and powerful, there are wicked men who are poor, not necessarily because of the wickedness of the rich, but because of their own wickedness: laziness, irresponsibility, self-indulgence, immorality. The wicked who are poor have their own schemes for diverting God's money from his purposes into their pockets.

Jesus tells us that we run another risk by being part of the world. "If you belonged to the world, the world would love you as its own. Because you do not belong to the world, but I have chosen you out of the world—therefore the world hates you" (Jn. 15:19). Some men and women will persecute us simply because we're Christians. If economic conditions worsen, persecution can be expected to increase. Are Christians going to be able to turn for help to those who hate and persecute them now? It's not likely. Will economic difficulties improve our chances of keeping tax exemptions which are now legal? Probably not. Will church-affiliated schools be looked upon more kindly? Probably less kindly. In difficult times our hope is not in the world but in the name of the Lord and in one another.

Even with all the risks, God, who loves us very much, tells us to remain involved in the world and its structures.

I am not asking you to take them out of the world, but I ask you to protect them from the evil one. They do not belong to the world, just as I do not belong to the world. Sanctify them in the truth; your word is truth. As you have sent me into the world, so I have sent them into the world (Jn. 17:15–18).

For the Lord's sake accept the authority of every human institution, whether of the emperor as supreme, or of governors, as sent by him to punish those who do wrong and to praise those who do right. For it is God's will that by doing right you should silence the ignorance of the foolish. As servants of God, live as free people, yet do not use your freedom as a pretext for evil. Honor everyone. Love the family of believers. Fear God. Honor the emperor (1 Pt. 2:13–17).

Another reason for Christians' involvement in the world is a strategic one. We want to bring the good news of salvation to all people, in order to deliver them from the kingdom of darkness and to bring them into the kingdom of light, thus to build the kingdom of Christ on earth. "You are the light of the world. A city built on a hill cannot be hid. No one after lighting a lamp puts it under the bushel basket, but on the lampstand, and it gives light to all in the house. In the same way, let your light shine before others, so that they may see your good works and give glory to your Father in heaven" (Mt. 5:14–16). We must be involved with people if we are to reach them. They must be able, at least, to see our good works.

Because of the complex nature of the 20th century, to be involved in the world means to rely heavily on its systems. We are in the thick of it, up to our eyebrows, and that is the position that God wants us to be in. However, we need to protect ourselves from being at a disadvantage if times worsen. Being provident in the face of the current situation means working toward a position in which we can prudently combine a measure of economic independence, opportunities for effective evangelism and opportunities for cooperating with God's overall plan for providing for mankind's needs.

CHAPTER FIVE

God's Work Comes First

THE THIRD PRINCIPLE is that God's provision has a twofold purpose: first, to give us enough resources to enable us to support his work and, second, to provide for our sustenance. He calls us to put his work first.

> The point is this: the one who sows sparingly will also reap sparingly, and the one who sows bountifully will also reap bountifully. Each of you must give as you have made up your mind, not reluctantly or under compulsion, for God loves a cheerful giver. And God is able to provide you with every blessing in abundance, so that by always having enough of everything you may share abundantly in every good work. As it is written,
>
> > He scatters abroad, he gives to the poor;
> > his righteousness endures forever.
>
> He who supplies seed to the sower and bread for food will supply and multiply your seed for sowing and increase the harvest of your righteousness. You will be enriched in every way for your great generosity, which will produce thanksgiving to God through us (2 Cor. 9:6–11).

Paul is telling us that God provides us with money to live on and money to give away; we don't have to choose between the two. The New Revised Standard Version's rendering of the final verse implies that God will enrich us in return for our generosity. A better way to understand the passage is to say that God will enrich us to enable us to give more generously. As God looks over the whole earth and what he wants to accomplish, he looks for men and women who will use money for his purposes. When he finds them he gives money to them.

Another implication of this principle is that in every paycheck, regardless of how small it may seem, there are two parts: one for our sustenance, the other for good works. Good works do not come out of our excess. What is left over after we provide for God's work will be sufficient for our needs. If you've used your whole paycheck for yourself, God could legitimately take back the part that you should have used for him.

Recognizing the two purposes in God's provision, we also see a difference in their priorities. "But strive first for the kingdom of God and his righteousness, and all these things will be given to you as well" (Mt. 6:33). We want first of all to put our funds into building God's dwelling place among men, and second into insulation for our own houses (see Hg. 1:2-4).

But what happens when times get harder and it's more difficult to support God's work? "In the presence of God and of Christ Jesus, who is to judge the living and the dead, and in view of his appearing and his kingdom, I solemnly urge you: proclaim the message; be persistent whether the time is favorable or unfavorable" (2 Tm. 4:1-2). When you think you can afford it and when you think you can't, when times are good and when times are bad—no matter what—be engaged in preaching the word and supporting apostolic work. We need to be engaged in God's work, regardless of the state of the economy. In fact, while we can afford it and while times are good, we want to set aside some of our resources for the days when it will be more difficult to fund God's work (see 1 Cor. 16:1-3).

If hard times come upon us, we are commanded to be ready to sacrifice our material well-being rather than to abandon God's work. Consider the Christians in Macedonia, whom Paul holds up as an example of generous giving.

> We want you to know, brothers and sisters, about the grace of God that has been granted to the churches of Macedonia, for during a severe ordeal of affliction, their abundant joy and their extreme poverty have overflowed in a wealth of generosity on their part. For, as I can testify, they voluntarily gave according to their means, and even beyond their means, begging us earnestly for the privilege of sharing in this ministry to the saints (2 Cor. 8:1-4).

The only thing they had in abundance was their joy, but they gave beyond their means, even begging for the privilege of giving. That is the kind of people we want to be, giving past the point of hurting, for the sake of God's work.

God assures us that, as we spend money now for his purposes, we will be repaid in the days to come. We can gladly endure suffering, hardship and privation in these days, knowing of God's promise.

What are the good works which Scripture calls us to support financially? First, we are to support the work of the elders, especially those who rule well and those who work in preaching and teaching (see 1 Tm. 5:17-18), along with those who do missionary work (see Ph. 4:14-18). We should be giving regularly to our church, fellowship or Christian community. The pastors of our churches and communities need to be supported so that they can continue the work God has given them. The church and its work, its mission and apostolate, need to be supported.

We are also enjoined to show hospitality to strangers and to support widows, orphans and those who are poor through no fault of their own (see 1 Tm. 5:3-9; Rm. 15:26). Almsgiving is something that Jesus urges upon us; it has always been a part of the life of the Christian people. An elder in the early church encouraged his people to almsgiving and works of mercy with these words:

> Almsgiving embraces under the single name of mercy many excellent works of devotion, so that the good intentions of all the faithful may be of equal value, even where their means are not. The love that we owe both

31

God and man is always free from any obstacle that would prevent us from having a good intention. The angels sang: "Glory to God in the highest, and peace to his people on earth." The person who shows love and compassion to those in any kind of affliction is blessed, not only with the virtue of good will but also with the gift of peace.

The works of mercy are innumerable. Their very variety brings this advantage to those who are true Christians, that in the matter of almsgiving not only the rich and affluent but also those of average means and the poor are able to play their part. Those who are unequal in their capacity to give can be equal in the love within their hearts (Leo the Great, sixth Lenten sermon, PL 54:287).

Almsgiving is not simply "do-goodism." It is part of the work of God, and it is spiritual. A man I know who spent some time in India said that everywhere he went things were very bad. Not only was there great poverty, sickness and suffering, but there also seemed to be a great spiritual depression across the land. It affected him so much that, although he was in a country which he would probably never be able to visit again, he simply could not bring himself to take pictures. He didn't want to remember any of it. He was able, though, to visit the place where Mother Teresa and her associates were ministering to the poor and sick. He found that there people were smiling. He was confronting a new spiritual reality. God was ministering to the poor through his people, bringing his own Spirit into the situation.

CHAPTER SIX

Prepare for Change

THE FOURTH PRINCIPLE is that we should always live in a way that prepares us for economic change. Scripture and ordinary human experience unite to tell us that economic conditions do change. "In the time of plenty think of the time of hunger; in days of wealth think of poverty and need. From morning to evening conditions change; all things move swiftly before the Lord" (Sir. 18:25-26). Throughout history, circumstances of varying degrees of gravity have brought about significant economic changes for the worse. Seasonal changes, inflationary trends, shifts in trade patterns, depression, famine, plague, war—things quickly go from good to bad. Most of us grew up expecting things to change, certainly, but only for the good! The gross national product is supposed to increase; salaries are supposed to go up; the consumer price index is supposed to go down. Our approach to the future is often unrealistic and, consequently, irresponsible.

In America, generally speaking, the 1970s and the 1980s were times of plenty. Scripture warns us that it is in just such times as these that we should recall times of hunger, times of poverty, times of need. The 1990s are proving to be uncertain times economically. Today's circumstances should remind us of scriptural admonitions to be cautious. "A prudent man sees danger and hides himself; but the simple go on, and suffer for it" (Pr. 22:3 RSV).

33

To live providently means to set aside a portion of today's plenty for tomorrow's need. To live resourcefully means to develop the skills and capabilities for producing and maintaining a larger proportion of the goods that are essential to our lives. "In the morning sow your seed, and at evening do not let your hands be idle [do your farmwork during the morning, but when you come home produce something else, engage in another trade]; for you do not know which will prosper" (Ec. 11:6). As we look toward the future, we are to be flexible, resourceful, able to do more than one thing to take care of our needs. Proverbs 31:13–25 provides us with the example of a provident and resourceful woman. She is flexible and knows a variety of skills to meet changing times. If we approach our economic future providently and resourcefully, we, like the woman in Proverbs 31, will be clothed in "strength and dignity." We, too, will be in a position to laugh at the time to come (v. 25).

Right about now you might find yourself becoming a little uneasy with this approach. What about living by faith? Doesn't Scripture forbid the laying up of treasures? Isn't this actually relying more on human efforts than on God's?

These are all good questions. Many well-intentioned, devout and intelligent Christians have looked at the same texts and come up with different understandings of them. These are also difficult questions. However, my interpretation is not a new one. These principles—people have a responsibility to care for themselves, they can possess material goods, they can own more than they need at the present moment—have been held by the majority of Christian teachers throughout the centuries (for example, Aquinas, Luther, Calvin, the social encyclicals of the Catholic Church, etc.). At the same time, this teaching acknowledges our complete dependence upon God and points out the dangers inherent in the possession and use of material goods.

This brings us to the fifth principle: As we prepare for the future, we must heed Scripture's warnings about the temptations that can besiege the person intent on pursuing and possessing wealth. These temptations include temptations to excessive solicitude (anxiety) for temporal goods, covetousness, idolatry, dishonesty and showing partiality to the rich. I will consider them in that order.

The first is anxiety.

> Therefore I tell you, do not worry about your life, what you will eat or what you will drink, or about your body, what you will wear. Is not life more than food, and the body more than clothing? Look at the birds of the air; they neither sow nor reap nor gather into barns, and yet your heavenly Father feeds them. Are you not of more value than they? And can any of you by worrying add a single hour to your span of life? And why do you worry about clothing? Consider the lilies of the field, how they grow; they neither toil nor spin, yet I tell you, even Solomon in all his glory was not clothed like one of these. But if God so clothes the grass of the field, which is alive today and tomorrow is thrown into the oven, will he not much more clothe you—you of little faith? Therefore do not worry, saying, "What will we eat?" or "What will we drink?" or "What will we wear?" For it is the Gentiles who strive for these things; and indeed your heavenly Father knows that you need all these things. But strive first for the kingdom of God and his righteousness, and all these things will be given to you as well. So do not worry about tomorrow, for tomorrow will bring worries of its own. Today's trouble is enough for today (Mt. 6:25–34).

"For everything there is a season, and a time for every matter under heaven" (Ec. 3:1). This passage can throw light on what Jesus means when he says, "Do not worry about tomorrow, for tomorrow will bring worries of its own. Today's trouble is enough for today." In summer you plan ahead for fall, and rightly so. If you start planning for the fall in midwinter, you are going too far. If you start planning today the things you should be planning tomorrow, you are being overly solicitous, overly concerned. So, as an admonition against this, the Lord reminds us of our Father's declared and demonstrated intent to provide for us.

The second danger is equally clear.

And he said to them, "Take care! Be on your guard against all kinds of greed; for one's life does not consist in the abundance of possessions." Then he told them a parable: "The land of a rich man produced abundantly. And he thought to himself 'What should I do, for I have no place to store my crops?' Then he said, 'I will do this: I will pull down my barns and build larger ones, and there I will store all my grain and my goods. And I will say to my soul, 'Soul, you have ample goods laid up for many years; relax, eat, drink, be merry.' But God said to him, 'You fool! This very night your life is being demanded of you. And the things you have prepared, whose will they be?' So it is with those who store up treasures for themselves, but are not rich toward God" (Lk. 12:15–21).

The key to understanding the last verse is the first—"Be on your guard against all kinds of greed." Greed and covetousness, which is the excessive love of possessions, are what Jesus condemned, not the laying up of provisions. In God's economy, riches are to be used, not held.

A man "stores up treasures" for himself if he acquires and obtains them simply because he likes possessing them. A man is rich toward God if he acquires and holds his goods for the right time in order to use them for God's purposes.

"He who contributes, [let him do so] in liberality" (Rm. 12:8 RSV). "In liberality" means openhandedly, freely, but also intelligently, not wastefully. A wise man does not give everything away just as soon as it comes into his hands. Being prodigal might seem better than being covetous, because you are not holding on to things, but what is really required is liberality, giving things away when they will do the most good.

As we make provision for the future, we should do so according to three criteria: sufficiency, contentment and proportion. Applying the criterion of sufficiency helps us to gauge whether we are providing too much or too little. What is needed is an amount adequate to the task, but no more. Obviously the person who is responsible for a large family will have to put away more goods than single persons responsible only for themselves. What is important is not that one is a larger amount than the other, but that both are sufficient.

Contentment is the wisdom to balance our needs against our desires. St. Paul urges us to be contented with having our basic needs met, rather than to desire things beyond our needs (1 Tm. 6:6–8). Often our desires far outstrip our needs, and we find ourselves discontented. Contentment comes from living simply, within our means.

Proportion, the last criterion, is the wisdom to live on a realistic economic level with regard to the times. Because times change, we might need more money simply to eat decently at one time than another. Sometimes we will need more for housing than we do at other times. What we possess should be in proportion to the times and in proportion to what we need in order to discharge our responsibilities to the Lord, to our families and to society.

These three criteria will act as safeguards against covetousness.

The third danger is idolatry.

> No one can serve two masters; for a slave will either hate the one and love the other, or be devoted to the one and despise the other. You cannot serve God and wealth (Mt. 6:24).

Fear or panic may tempt us to turn away from the one true God, and turn idolatrously to wealth (material possessions) for protection and deliverance. One antidote to this danger is to get our loyalties straight so that fear and panic won't affect us. We must declare ourselves loyal only to God, and renounce any shred of idolatry within ourselves. Another antidote is to make adequate provision, which wards off panic.

Sometimes it is difficult for us to see others getting rich dishonestly and not be tempted to do the same. Dishonesty is the fourth danger we face.

> But as for me, my feet had almost stumbled;
>   my steps had nearly slipped.
> For I was envious of the arrogant;
>   I saw the prosperity of the wicked (Ps. 73:2–3).

The psalmist admits that he came very close to stumbling. If you think you stand firm, take heed. You will be tempted to be dishonest in all sorts of ways. Be on guard.

The fifth warning also cuts close to the bone.

> My brothers and sisters, do you with your acts of favoritism really believe in our glorious Lord Jesus Christ? For if a person with gold rings and in fine clothes comes into your assembly, and if a poor person in dirty clothes also comes in, and if you take notice of the one wearing the fine clothes and say, "Have a seat here, please," while to the one who is poor you say, "Stand there," or, "Sit at my feet," have you not made distinctions among yourselves, and become judges with evil thoughts? (Jas. 2:1–4).

If times get worse, we may be tempted to show partiality toward the rich among our brothers. Motivated by desire for gain or security, we might think, If I'm nice to him, he'll take care of me. Why be nice to that other fellow? He can't help me.

Scripture warns us against this temptation, precisely because it is one to which we can fall prey.

As I said at the beginning, the one unchanging fact of life is the fact of change itself. We are surrounded by tremendously rapid changes, yet we often act as if the economic future will not change, at least not for the worse. Being provident and resourceful means being realistic about the future and being prepared for what might come. As we prepare ourselves, we must be on the watch for anxiety, covetousness, idolatry, dishonesty and partiality toward the rich. These are all real dangers for each one of us, but we should not shrink from our responsibilities simply because of the dangers.

CHAPTER SEVEN

Applying the Principles

ECONOMICS, MONEY, FINANCES, the possession and distribution of goods—all figure importantly in our lives as Christians. God's point of view on these things, as revealed in Scripture and Christian teaching, is found in the principles we have discussed. We have no lasting city here. While we are here, though, we need to relate to economic systems and structures as part of God's way of providing for all his creatures. We can neither ignore these structures nor retreat from them. His provision for us through these systems has a twofold purpose: to give us sustenance and to give us the wherewithal to support his work. Of the two, his work comes first. It is, then, crucial for God's plan that we be good stewards of our financial resources, prepared to adjust to financial change, and aware of the constant danger that material goods and money present for Christians. However, these dangers should not prompt us to retreat from our responsibility, since God has promised us his own strength in dealing with such temptations.

The principles we have considered are intended to form our minds and attitudes, to give us a biblical perspective. Speaking of them as "forming" our minds and giving us "perspective" indicates that they will teach us *how* to think about money, possessions and so forth, but not teach us *what* to think. What we think will be determined to a large extent by the actual situation we face.

Three elements of the current situation were highlighted in the opening chapters of this book. First of all, life in our society has undergone massive change in recent years. Part of this change is noticeable in the new set of ideals and values presented to us. We are being told that happiness is a matter of ease and comfort, of doing what we want. The things which free us from other obligations—for example, labor-saving appliances—and which give us the time for ease are not themselves free. Also, those things which make our free time meaningful cost money. Work and money, therefore, have become primarily means to ease and comfort.

Second, and most important, a change has been worked in our character by this desire for ease and comfort. Once self-reliant, strong, provident and resourceful, our characters have been significantly weakened by a life of ease. Each year finds more of us dependent, weak, improvident and unresourceful.

For many, happiness rests entirely upon the promises of the economic system. If the system were to fail, they would be lost; the meaning of their lives would evaporate. Many are also dependent upon the system for all the necessities of their lives because they despise hard work and lack the skills necessary to approach self-sufficiency. They are weak because they have selected ease and comfort as their ideals.

These elements have brought with them a kind of selfish individualism. One's concern is only for one's own enjoyment, pleasure and personal ends. This individualism, coupled with the desire for pleasure, generates a radical selfishness. Commentators have pointed out that the typical American family exhibits the kind of selfish individualism that moves people away from cooperation and a shared life. The typical family has a phone, car, television, VCR, many large and small appliances and a host of other possessions. Often husband and wife will have their own cars and VCRs so that each can do what he or she wants, independently.

It is usually considered desirable that children have their own rooms. Most middle-class children don't have to share rooms. As they grow older and conflicts arise over what to watch on television, parents often buy them their own televisions. The same thing happens when they begin to use the phone and when they begin to drive. Each person is equipped with his own things to satisfy his own desires. This type of life-style breeds self-centeredness and makes it virtually impossible for children to learn anything about the give and take of social life, of postponing their desires, or of sharing their lives with other people.

Of all the fields of learning, none gives a better rationale for this individualistic, pleasure-oriented life-style than modern psychology. Modern psychology is the philosophy of our time. It is the most popular subject on university campuses. In the U.S., it is estimated that 80 percent of college students take at least one psychology course during their studies. A visit to any bookstore will show the great demand for books on psychology. Modern psychology clearly sanctions the hedonistic life-style which has developed in the West over the last century. Some argue that it has not only sanctioned but also helped to cause it.

A good deal of current psychological literature is taken up with remedies for the problems caused by modern pleasure-oriented society. The reason? Much of what the psychological theories encourage has come to be itself a great source of psychological problems. Professor Donald T. Campbell of the University of Wisconsin has spoken on the great danger of the psychological approach. In his August 31, 1975, presidential address to the American Psychological Association, Campbell said that

> the religions of all ancient urban civilizations taught that many aspects of human nature . . . for example, lust, wrath . . . need to be curbed [if social life is to work well]. Psychology and psychiatry, on the other hand, not only describe man as selfishly motivated, but implicitly or explicitly teach that he ought to be so. They tend to see repression and inhibition of individual impulse as undesirable, and to see all guilt as a . . . neurotic blight created by cruel child-rearing and a needlessly repressive society, recommending that we accept our biological

41

and psychological impulses as good and seek pleasure rather than enchain ourselves with duty.

Campbell went on to argue that the ancient way is by far the better and, indeed, the more scientific. The modern way, he maintained, is likely to lead to social and psychological chaos.

The effect of these changes on our characters is the most serious thing we have to face. It is much more serious than either the new ideals of economic life or the weaknesses which we find in the economic system itself. Changes in systems and ideals are one thing; changes in people are quite another.

Third, we must deal with a new kind of economic vulnerability present in the current economic system. The problem is not simply one of escalating prices. The entire monetary exchange and trade system needs to be overhauled if it is to handle the realities of modern economic life adequately. We are operating with a monetary system which has no real foundation; money itself has become a commodity. Trade levels are too high to be sustained by the mechanisms presently available in the world's economic system. Geopolitical stresses and strains caused or aggravated by the difficulties inherent in the system threaten us with political and economic instability, if not war.

In our daily lives, this economic vulnerability threatens such necessities of life as housing, energy, food, clothing, medical care and transportation. These are essentials for contemporary social life and yet the system cannot provide them at a reasonable price, nor in a consistent manner.

Thus we are triply cursed: we seek an ideal happiness which only the economy can supply; the economy, for its part, has difficulty even supplying the necessities of life, let alone happiness. The ideal we have accepted has sufficiently weakened us that we are unable to care for ourselves adequately or to supplement what the economic system does provide. Applying scriptural principles will provide a way out of this dilemma and offer us a way of responding to our present situation.

The first result of applying these principles should be the

recovery of a personal character which is provident and resourceful. We might decide to respond either to the ideal of ease and comfort, or to our own economic vulnerability, or even both together, but still not have addressed the question of personal character. Until we become provident and resourceful people, we will be unable to cope effectively with the other realities that confront us.

To do this we will need to achieve some distance from the economic system of this world in order to gain effective command over the material resources entrusted to us. We are much more thoroughly embedded in the economic system than we should be; too many of our values and attitudes have been twisted to fit into its mold. On the other hand, since God's plans can only be carried out by people of goodwill making right use of this system, we cannot seek to pull out, but must maintain a prudent involvement in this world system.

One way to achieve this distance and to gain more control over our economic resources is to cut back or to cut out purchases on revolving charge accounts. The use of these accounts plunges us into the heart of the system, and penalizes us through higher costs. Buying things on a cash basis returns us to a more direct, simple and ultimately more moral economics. Other positive responses might include: getting more involved in your business or work, if by doing so the company could better serve its clients or would be a better place for its employees; learning marketable skills which would allow you to take another job if your present one terminated or if you needed additional income; learning how to maintain and repair your home, appliances and tools so that you would be less dependent on the repairman and could save money besides. A number of families, a church or a fellowship located in a city might get involved in collective gardening or purchase a farm. Such a venture would allow them to become more self-sufficient with regard to their food supply and would help them develop useful skills.

Keeping some distance from the economic system will help us gain effective command of many of our material resources. We are vulnerable to those who direct the system to the degree that they command our resources. If everything we own has been purchased on borrowed money or on credit, then we are not in command of it; the lender or credit company is in command. This situation can be of great difficulty in times of economic emergency: our cars, our homes, our possessions could be taken from us. Further, not being able to command our own resources can cripple us when it comes to doing the Lord's will or answering his call. A church which depends financially upon the donations of a company which is unjust or uses immoral advertising is not in a position to criticize that injustice or immorality. An individual who has his goods tied up as collateral for loans may be unable to answer a call to the missions.

We also need to look for the signs of the coming times and plan accordingly. If we knew the events of the next 20 years with certainty, we would be in an excellent position to plan ahead. Of course, we do not know the future. The position we are in calls for a careful analysis of the circumstances which might await us in the near future, perhaps the next six months, and for a high degree of flexibility in our planning. The economic future is, at best, unstable and dangerous. It might turn out that all the gloomy doomsday prognostications are wrong—the economy may just limp along without seriously dislocating any of us. Or it could (although this is highly unlikely) get markedly better for a long period of time.

As I worked on this book, I had the opportunity to read a lot written by futurologists. Futurologists are thoughtful persons who study the past and the present and try to make some determination of the future. This is not just guesswork; a lot of weight is given to their conclusions by large corporations and the military. Among futurologists there is a saying: The future will always be different from what you thought it would be. As we consider our responsibilities and try to discover what to do, it would be a mistake to build all our plans around only one specific set of eventualities. We need to be flexible. We should strive to be able to respond well to a number of possible futures. Imagine yourself as a boxer, on your toes, able to move in a number of different directions.

A driver on a dark road relies on his headlights to see

down the road. He needs to control his speed, so that he's able to respond to what the lights illumine, and not outrun them. The driver can't see all the way down the road, but he has to see far enough ahead to be able to adjust to the next turn. Reliable economic predictors will not enable us to see very far at all, but perhaps far enough to be prepared for the next six months. If we stay prepared for likely events in the upcoming six months, we will be in a better position to handle whatever comes our way.

Applying scriptural principles to the elements of modern economic life which concern us has given us four fundamental responses to our current situation.

1. Develop the character of a provident and resourceful person; train ourselves according to such values and recover such a way of life.

2. Achieve some distance from the economic system of this world; be less involved in the system and less dependent upon its rewards and punishments.

3. Gain effective command over the material resources entrusted to us; use our money wisely; budget, save and avoid credit purchases.

4. Develop a flexible plan for the next six months.

What follows will show how to make these responses a practical reality in our lives.

CHAPTER EIGHT

Testing Your Character

EVERYTHING WE HAVE TALKED ABOUT SO FAR points to the importance of developing a provident and resourceful character or personality for those who wish to negotiate successfully the uncertain economic times in which we live. How can a person judge whether he or she has such a character? Each of us is provident and resourceful in one way or another. Most of us have some method of budgeting and could give an account of where our money goes. We probably are not too strung out on credit, although we might be strung out a lot more than we wish. We probably have some kind of savings, or are working on it. Each of these things—budgeting, credit and savings—is a key to provident and resourceful living. However, we need to assess something deeper—our character.

How would you handle living in tougher times? If you couldn't have the house or office at 70 degrees all day, if you couldn't use the car, if you couldn't use the refrigerator, if you couldn't use your dishwasher, if your stove wasn't working, how would you fare? Could you find the emotional strength to keep on an even keel, or would you be jumpy and generally disagreeable? Do you have enough confidence in your ability to provide for yourself and others—your children or your parents—so that you wouldn't be consumed with anxiety and worry in difficult times?

Many of us have lived or are living in ways that test our

47

self-reliance and internal strength. As a result, we are becoming more provident and resourceful people. Others of us, however, have not lived this way and are probably somewhat concerned about how we would perform under trying circumstances. For those of us who have these kinds of doubts, the Self-Sufficiency Exercise will prove helpful. This exercise has many benefits: it allows us to test how we would perform under moderately trying circumstances; it tests the state of our preparedness for unforeseen economic difficulties; it gives us a feel for what the future might hold.

Fundamentally, the Self-Sufficiency Exercise consists of living for a certain period of time (at least two or three days, but a week is better) as if all the external energy supplied to your house — gas, electricity, gasoline — were unavailable. If your household appliances are powered by propane, as they are in many rural areas, they can be used during the exercise, since propane is readily stored and does not require continuous supply from the outside. If you use electricity or natural gas, though, it will mean not using your kitchen stove, furnace, electric lights, refrigerator, freezer, etc. Living like this for a weekend or a week can be very instructive.

While the exercise should be a significant test of your situation, it should not impair anyone's health or safety. If it is cold and you have small children or older adults living with you, the heat could be turned down, but not off. If people have special dietary needs which necessitate refrigeration or the cooking of food, then their needs should be taken care of. Water should be readily available — although I would suggest using the outside rather than inside taps — and toilets should be used. The exercise should be carried out thoughtfully, with an eye to the health and safety of those involved.

It is important that the exercise be carried out for a sufficiently long period of time. If the time is too short, the experience could end up more like a party than a real test of how to live under trying circumstances. When I first decided to do this, I talked to two neighbor families and we decided to do the exercise together over a weekend. We pooled our equipment and made a common schedule, sharing meals, recreation and so on. Two of us had birthdays over that weekend and we decided to celebrate them as part of the exercise. My wife baked a cake in a solar oven made out of a potato chip box (it was delicious); we had picnic meals in the back yard (it was summer); and we had bonfires at night with group singing, storytelling and skits. We had a great time, but we had too much fun. If it had been real, we would not have been partying and picnicking the whole weekend. In fact, life would be pretty grim. Running the exercise with other families is valuable, but it needs to be for a longer time and with a less festive air. The next time, we did it during the work week, which approximated a normal routine more closely than a weekend in summer with two birthdays on it.

The first thing to do is to schedule a time for the Self-Sufficiency Exercise. The next thing is to assess your equipment needs. Since you will not be using the refrigerator or freezer (do not unplug them and ruin your food; just put a piece of masking tape across the door as a reminder not to open it), ask yourself if you have enough nonrefrigerated food on hand to provide meals for the duration of the exercise. This will raise many other questions. How dependent am I on refrigerated foods? Do I have food stored in case something like this happened unexpectedly? Are there ways in which I can keep milk and other foods cool without using electricity?

Next, look at your cooking requirements. During the exercise, will you eat only uncooked food? If this were for real, would you eat only uncooked food for a long period of time? Since you will not use your household stove, decide what you will use. Many woodburning stoves and kerosene heaters have cooking space on them. Having this kind of stove/heater and enough wood or kerosene would solve both your heating and cooking needs. Camp stoves can also be used. I would suggest the propane type rather than those that use liquid fuels (white gas, Coleman fuel, etc.,) since it is dangerous to have those fuels in your home around open flames, and camp stoves that use liquid fuels can flare up. If you use a propane camp stove, I would suggest that you buy the kind of propane tanks found on recreational vehicles and some home barbeques; you can keep the propane outside and run a hose from the tank to the stove as a desirable safety feature. Also, make sure that you have enough fire extinguishers to deal with any accidents.

Lighting is next. Flashlights have only a limited value since batteries will go dead. You will need some kind of lantern or fuel-fired lamp. Camp lanterns will do, but, again, propane is safer. The best are kerosene lamps that use mantles. They are highly reliable, produce the equivalent of a 60-watt light bulb, and are inexpensive to operate. Kerosene is a very safe fuel and can be used and stored inside since it has a very low flash point. Two or three of these lamps will probably be adequate. Kerosene lamps and camp lanterns are hot. They need to be used carefully, and children should only use them when guided by an adult.

If it is winter, you will need to be concerned about heat. Are there enough blankets or sleeping bags to keep everyone warm at night? Are there enough sweaters and coats for use during the day? Portable kerosene- or propane-fired heaters are good to use, as is a woodburning stove. Most fireplaces are very inefficient; in most homes they actually take heat out of the house rather than put it in. While you are thinking about your heating needs, you should think about the ability of your home to hold the heat. Is the insulation sufficient? Are the windows caulked? Are your storm windows adequate or do they need replacement?

Transportation is an important part of our life. We are used to being able to hop in a car and get across town in a matter of minutes. Our schedules and our workday are often built around the possibility of quick transportation. During this exercise, it is useful to reduce the use of your car to a minimum. Bicycling, walking and public transportation should be used as alternatives.

You also need to consider how washing will be done. Without the hot-water heater or dishwasher, how will dishes be cleaned? Do you have buckets or pots large enough to heat water? What about laundry? How will people take care of their personal hygiene? Those who have gone camping have had experience in providing for these needs, but the questions should be asked afresh. Since much of the exercise parallels the kinds of things people do when they camp, it is easy to think that this will be just like camping. Although there are similarities, doing these things on vacation, out in the woods, has the sense of fun and festivity. Living like this in your own home, where you are used to turning on the light, setting the thermostat, cooking on a kitchen stove, etc., is not nearly as much fun.

Sitting around in a dark, cold house is not much fun, either. What will be the tone of life during the exercise? How do you want to experience it? What will your family do during the free time? It is worth planning some games or entertainment. Music, singing, reading aloud and playing games are all helpful in keeping people's spirits up.

Just preparing for this exercise will point out how much we depend on timesaving, low-cost appliances: refrigerators, freezers, stoves, dishwashers, televisions, radios, heaters, furnaces and so on. Doing the exercise will probably mean purchasing some equipment and fuel, which will force you to reallocate some of the money in your budget.

The following checklist will help you plan the exercise.

—Food: no refrigerated foods; need dried or canned milk, canned food, fresh vegetables and fruits.

—Cooking: no kitchen stove unless it is propane; woodburning stove or kerosene heater/stove or camp stoves, preferably propane.

—Lights: no electric lights; need flashlights, kerosene lamps or camp lanterns. Again, propane is recommended.

—Safety: fire extinguishers.

—Water: no inside taps; need water containers to store water in the home.

—Heat: no electric or natural gas heaters/furnace; need woodburning stoves, portable kerosene or propane stoves; also need warm bedding and clothing.

—Transportation: use car as little as possible; substitute bicycling, walking or public transportation.

—Entertainment: plan games, music or some other kind of recreation.

—Equipment: ask where you will get this equipment. Will

you borrow it? If you purchase it, you need to ask where you will get the money.

— Schedule: figure out time and notify all concerned.

Such an exercise can teach you a lot, both about your state of preparedness and about your character. It can also tell you about the strengths and weaknesses in your family relationships. What you learn can be very helpful in making progress toward provident and resourceful living.

In August, 1992, millions of people were forced into living without the usual comforts of civilization when Hurricane Andrew slammed into heavily populated Dade County, Florida, severely damaging or destroying 72,000 homes. The 140-mph winds (gusts to 164 mph) left 1.8 million Floridians without power. Because of advance warning and a well-executed evacuation plan, only 13 people were killed in Florida. Another person was killed in Louisiana when Andrew made a second 140-mph onslaught there. All told, Andrew caused $20 billion damage, making it the costliest disaster in U.S. history up to that time.

How many of these people were prepared for the hardships they were to face?

As you watched the news reports and interviews, you probably noticed vast differences in the reactions of those whose possessions had been ripped away from them. Some seemed utterly incapable of even comprehending what had happened or what they were going to do next. Others were taking the disaster in stride. Sure, it was a tragedy, but let's get going on the reconstruction of our normal life.

Many people reported that their priorities had shifted somewhat — the loss of everything they owned had revealed to them that what really counted were their lives and the lives of the ones they loved. I suspect that from now on these insights will help guide many of these people to a more provident and resourceful approach to life.

CHAPTER NINE

Purchasing on Credit

REDUCING YOUR VULNERABILITY to credit institutions is an important part of getting control of your own economic resources and achieving some distance from certain negative features of the world's economic system. In many ways the advent of credit as the normal means of making purchases has been one of the most profound events in the economic history of the United States. Since it is so important, we need to deal with it in a thorough and practical way. Dealing with the impact of credit on our lives should be one of our highest priorities.

As I mentioned in Chapter One, money has changed from a substitute for products in a barter system to a product itself. Credit is nothing more than renting money. Sometimes, in preference to renting a product, we rent money, so we can buy the product. We may end up paying for the money long after we have used up or worn out the product. With a rental agreement we may have recourse if the property proves unsatisfactory, but we have little recourse if the money we rent doesn't buy us what we wanted.

Most of our credit education has come from banks and financial institutions who want us to rent money from them, from retailers who are willing to get into the lending business in order to sell their products, and from our government, which shows us the way through its own deficit spending.

We are always hearing expressions such as, "Buy now, pay later" or "Take up to 36 months to pay." We have begun to accept as a fact that there is no need to wait for what we want. No one advertises with the slogan, "Save now, buy later."

Before buying on credit we should consider some alternatives. Besides doing without the intended purchase—the simplest option—we could consider whether we could borrow the thing we want, whether there are people who could responsibly share ownership with us, or whether we could benefit from renting it. The answers to these questions will depend on what we want or need, why we want or need it, where we live and whom we know. Friends who live in the same neighborhood have countless opportunities for pooling equipment. We might decide to rent or lease something we need, depending on our resources. There are places that specialize in renting almost anything; for one-time use, we would do well to check on such an alternative.

We might decide to pay cash rather than buy on credit. There is a real cost to buying on credit: we pay for it in the resulting markup of the product, or in the finance charges, or both. Many who extend credit raise their prices to pass on to their customers the cost of this privilege. We should find out what the annual percentage rate (APR) will be. This is the rate of interest paid in the course of one year on the amount of money we borrow. By comparing APRs shown by different lenders or merchants, we may find that we can get our money cheaper elsewhere. Or perhaps we will decide that, rather than pay $175 for a $100 item, we could do without it until we can save the $100.

The important point here is to realize and exercise our freedom. We do have a choice and we may choose not to buy on credit.

If I were to develop a range of "probably acceptable" to "probably unacceptable" items to buy on credit, housing would be on the acceptable end. On the other end would be those objects which have no lasting value and which could not be listed as assets. Included in this list would be vacations, groceries, drugstore sundries and other nondurable goods. It is generally imprudent to buy on credit something we will not possess, like a vacation. It is equally imprudent to buy on credit something we will no longer have when it is paid for, like a bottle of shampoo. There are exceptions, like medical emergencies, for which we must sometimes borrow money. However, you may find that the doctor or hospital will allow you to work out a no-interest payment plan with them directly.

Credit cards are often helpful means of identification, but we should make a rational choice about using them to charge a purchase to our account. If we intend simply to pay for the item when the bill comes in, are we sure we will have the money available at that time? If we intend to pay finance charges, is the item worth the price we will end up paying? After we start adding up the real cost, we may just come up with a better way to get what we need. If we don't need it, why pay for it? If we are buying on credit because we can't afford the item, we should consider not buying it at all. If we can't afford it, and it can't be borrowed, rented or substituted for, perhaps we can talk ourselves out of wanting it. Madison Avenue, the mythological source of advertising, entices us to want what it wants to sell. We can say no to advertising enticements and to so-called easy-payment plans, and later find ourselves with money for other purposes.

Some see installment credit as a means of enforced savings. "If I borrow the money, I'll have to pay it back, but if I take it out of savings I won't put it back." If you find it difficult to pay back your savings, get someone to help you. Set up a payroll-deduction plan or have someone hold you accountable for it.

Another argument for buying on credit is to bet on increasing inflation. This is sometimes referred to as "paying it back with cheaper dollars." The idea is this: If the item you bought today for $1,000 sells for $1,400 by the time you finish paying for it, and you paid less than $1,400 including finance charges, you came out ahead. This argument is based on three assumptions. It relies on continuing inflation, on your continuing to work and/or having money to invest, and on your income increasing at or above the rate of inflation. These plans have worked out fine for some people, but not so well for those on a fixed income or those who get laid off. Besides, the early '90s were a classic example of how interest rates and inflation rates will fluctuate.

What about buying a car on credit, or a bedroom suite or appliances? One measure of whether or not to buy something on credit is whether the article being purchased will appreciate or depreciate in value while you pay for it. Houses usually appreciate in value. Cars depreciate, and so do furniture and appliances. Some things have no resale value at all when you are done paying for them; some have long since worn out. A good rule of thumb is not to buy on credit anything that will be unusable when it is paid for. Cars, especially new ones, usually have some value after the loan is paid in full, unless you buy a used car financed by a loan shark. Cars are often a necessity directly related to work, which may mean you must buy one. However, you might look into leasing as an alternative to buying.

The possible savings one could have with leasing are derived from the fact that the leasing company gets a lower price by volume car buying and passes that savings on to its customers. Also, if you are leasing the car for your business, there is a possible tax write-off. The problem is that the leasing company may write into your contract that you must buy the car at the end of your lease, which would probably wipe out any savings you had made. Leasing does not appear to be a sound alternative for an individual under these conditions. When the new car market is in decline, leasing conditions may be more favorable.

Acquiring furniture and appliances can often demand a lot of resourcefulness. One alternative is to rent a furnished apartment while saving for and acquiring furniture gradually. Furniture can be bought used and then refinished or reupholstered. Often, secondhand items can be borrowed or even received as gifts. Some couples prefer to start their families with inexpensive furniture and buy nicer things when the children are grown. In general, borrowing should be at least a second choice. Measure the real cost of buying on credit. Will you have to give up groceries for a color television? Save for it instead of buying now and paying later. Then, if some emergency comes up, you will have money in the bank rather than a half-paid-for color television that you may not even be able to sell.

Some people think that borrowing for an education which will permanently raise their income is a good investment. However, it is only a good investment if they are sure that their income will increase. In a solid economy, a degree commands a higher income, but many students fail to finish their degree, or fail to train themselves for available employment. Those who have worked, even part-time, before making a decision to obtain more schooling may have a better idea of the job market than those who have concentrated all their attention on school.

What if an emergency does come up? Suppose you have to borrow? Where should you do it? The cheapest loans are usually obtained from family members at no interest. Such loans are notoriously bad for relationships. Problems arise in the absence of written agreements, when both parties have mismatched expectations for repayment and when the loan becomes the focal point of the relationship. The next least expensive way is to borrow from your insurance company against the cash value of your life insurance. (Not all life insurance has cash value.) If you die, the amount of your loan would be deducted from the payment of your insurance. Credit unions, if you are eligible, can give the next best rates, then banks or savings banks, then a dealer financed through a bank, then a dealer financed through a finance company, then the finance company, and, last, the loan shark.

Finance companies and loan sharks make their product appealing by making the payment amount so small as to seem attainable. Fifty or 100 dollars a month doesn't sound so bad until you realize you will pay it for the rest of your life. Finance companies also tend to place a lien on more than the thing you want to buy, often through a second mortgage on your house and/or a chattel mortgage on all your personal property. Defaulting on a loan to a finance company is usually more costly than defaulting to a bank.

Getting into debt is serious business; don't do it without considerable research. An argument can be made for borrowing for a car, and there are times when it is better to borrow than to take from savings. If your savings is a timed deposit and you would pay a $100 penalty or lose all the interest for the quarter by withdrawing it, and if that penalty or interest exceeded the amount of interest you would have to pay for a loan, then it would be better to borrow. Some lending institutions promote borrowing against your savings as being cheaper because the rate is only two percent or so over the rate paid on your savings. They are not saying it's cheaper to borrow than to take it out of savings; they are only saying they can loan you the money cheaper than the bank across the street. In a sense, they will loan you your savings. With some institutions, however, the rate you pay may be higher than two percent over the savings rate. If on the other hand they are offering you something that will save you money, it is prudent not to wipe out your savings.

If you find yourself in debt now, you should begin taking action to get out of debt. Follow these steps:

1. Itemize your debts, to reflect the amounts, finance charges, source and payment schedule.

2. Discover ways to save.

3. Consider ways to raise your income.

4. In paying off interest-bearing debts, begin with those which are the most expensive. Consider both the amount of your monthly payment and the APR. For example, if you have two $1,000 debts, and suddenly you received a $1,000 gift, your future cash position would be helped more by paying off the one with the $100 per month payment than the one with the $50 per month payment. This assumes, of course, that the interest rates and the payment schedules are the same. It would not be true if the loan with the $50 payment only had two payments due, while the loan with the $100 payment had 18; or if one was at two percent while the other was at 22 percent.

5. If the bill collector is pounding on your door, talk to him. Don't be silent. Silence makes collectors nervous, and

when they're nervous they sometimes sue. Tell him how you plan to pay off your debt. If you're out of work, say so and tell him what you can do now (even if it's nothing) and what you'll do when you go to work again. Be sure to promise to do only what you can, and then do it, even if it's only five dollars per month. Lenders can be very reasonable if you show that you have good intentions; they may even forego some of their interest if you show signs of paying. A credit bureau or collection agency is likely to be less understanding because it won't be trying to keep you as a customer. Again, the truth is your best defense. Don't be afraid to challenge credit bureaus. They must show you what your record is; if it is wrong, they must correct it.

Exercise willpower by not adding more credit purchases. Since we must live with credit, it will pay to live prudently with it. It is normally realistic to buy only what we can afford. The less vulnerable we are to credit institutions, the freer we will be to use our money for the things we need.

Chapter Ten

Getting Control of Your Money

Managing your money could also be called "planned spending." Someone said that money management is a matter of being able to tell your money where you want it to go, rather than wondering where it went. It is an essential ingredient in a provident and resourceful way of life. While God calls some Christians in a special way to depend on him day by day, many others avoid the tedious task of managing their resources by claiming to trust in God. "God will take care of me," they say. "I don't need to oversee my money." This approach, however, flies in the face of the constant teaching of Scripture to exercise responsibility.

Scripture encourages us to be wise, to use our heads, to gain control over the things we are responsible for.

> By wisdom a house is built,
>   and by understanding it is established;
> by knowledge the rooms are filled
>   with all precious and pleasant riches.
> Wise warriors are mightier than strong ones,
>   and those who have knowledge than those who
>   have strength;
> for by wise guidance you can wage your war,

and in abundance of counselors there is victory.
Wisdom is too high for fools (Pr. 24:3–7a).

Scripture encourages us to take charge of our money in such a way that we will be prepared for the future. Not exercising this kind of oversight is a matter of laziness.

Go to the ant, you lazybones;
　　consider its ways, and be wise.
Without having any chief
　　or officer or ruler,
it prepares its food in summer,
　　and gathers its sustenance in harvest.
How long will you lie there, O lazybones?
　　When will you rise from your sleep?
A little sleep, a little slumber,
　　a little folding of the hands to rest,
and poverty will come upon you like a robber,
　　and want, like an armed warrior (Pr. 6:6–11).

The world around us tells us, "You earned your money. Now spend it any way you like and you will be happy." Scripture says that we will be content only if we have been faithful stewards.

There is no easy way to be a good steward. It takes work. Record-keeping is a tedious, joyless endeavor. The good news is that budgeting does work and that you can actually gain control over your resources. When you are in financial trouble and you have not managed your money carefully, there is always the nagging suspicion that something is wrong. As a result you live with a constant anxiety, not knowing where you stand, or when the axe will fall, or when the creditor will telephone. Without a budget, you are more likely to fall into the trap of spending money for less important items. Vagrants who spend what money they have on alcohol may have no money for food; you might spend your money eating out and not have enough for groceries, where the same money would buy more meals.

Here are some of the reasons for budgeting.

1. It is a tool for making us more provident and resourceful.

2. It will allow us to gain more control of our own financial resources.

3. It will help us to decide more carefully where we spend our money and thus free more of our resources for the work of God's kingdom.

4. It leads to more intelligent planning for other parts of our lives.

In approaching budgeting, there are three goals to aim for. The first is to gain control over your income and expenses. This is a result of applying the scriptural principles that we discussed earlier. The second goal is to get out of debt. Finally, you should develop a specific savings program to plan for such things as retirement, the replacement of appliances and other household equipment that cannot be repaired, educational expenses for the children, replacement of cars and so on. Saving for the future is an essential dimension of the provident life.

Money management means planning, and the place to begin is by reviewing your income. Are you in the right job with the right company? Are you receiving maximum return on your investments, savings and pension programs? If you need help in answering these questions, don't be afraid to consult some experts: "In abundance of counselors there is victory" (Pr. 24:6).

Review your expenses also. Begin by assembling your check stubs, old bills, receipts, credit statements and the records of personal allowances for members of your family. If you find that you have been erratic in saving these items, resolve to change. It helps to have separate places for storing due bills and receipts of payment. Some people use different envelopes or boxes. I use two different drawers in my desk. When bills come in, I store them in one drawer; when I pay them, I put the receipt or a record of payment in another drawer.

As you review your expenses, learn to distinguish between needs and wants. The ability to make this distinction, not only in looking at bills already paid but at the point of purchase, is essential. Until you can distinguish between what you want and what you really need, you will not be able to get control of your money. This distinction is difficult. Every desire can seem like a need; you must be honest with yourself. Christians can ask the Lord to discipline their desires. The alternative is poverty and disgrace for the one who rejects discipline (see Pr. 13:18).

Look at each of the major expenses confronting you and ask yourself some hard questions.

1. Shelter. Can we afford this house? Are the payments too high? Would we do better to sell it, take our equity and get a home more suited to our ability to pay?

2. Food. Is eating out eating up our budget? How much can be saved with menu planning? How much do we spend on the average, per person, per month, for food?

3. Clothing. Do we shop wisely? Are we behind because we buy cheap things that wear out quickly, which turns out to be more expensive in the long run? Do we shop around for sales? Are we open to buying used clothing?

4. Education. Can we afford these high tuition rates? Do the children need to go to nursery school? Is it wise that they are taking music lessons? Can we afford these lessons?

5. Transportation. Do we need more than one car? How much would be saved if we sold our best car? How can we cut driving by 20 percent?

6. Vacation. Are there less expensive alternatives? Do we have to leave town to have a vacation? Wouldn't camping be a good alternative this year?

The first step in budgeting is to identify current categories of expense, to examine the amount of each expense, the percentage of your income it represents, and the relative importance of each category of expense. Separate these into three columns.

1. Necessary, unavoidable items. This would include expenses for supporting God's work, housing, clothing, food, medical care, education, etc. Be careful what goes into these categories. Be sure that each item is a necessary expense in line with the gifts, responsibilities, resources and direction the Lord is giving you. If you have talent, music lessons may be a necessary educational expense. Two cars may also be better for transportation, but perhaps only one car is really necessary. Also check whether the level of expense can be cut back.

2. Future necessities. This includes funds for a new appliance if the old one is giving out, or money to replace the driveway that is breaking up or a car that is on its last legs, and so on. This is basically a category for saving. These items must be ranked, since it may not be possible to set money aside for all of them now.

3. Nice but not necessary items. These may be replacements for furniture, carpeting and the like, or added refinements to your life-style, or other items or experiences which can make life pleasant, but which are not essential.

Fill in all the categories under each of the columns until available funds give out. In the rare case where funds are available after the three columns are filled, consider investment opportunities. If you can pay all your bills and meet your savings goals, then still have 10 percent of your gross annual income left over, wise investment of some of your surplus funds is a valid consideration.

In a time of continuing inflation, always make your best estimate of an item of expense and add from five to 15 percent as a safety factor. Make sure that unforeseen expenses are really unforeseen, and not forgotten; be complete in your survey of upcoming expenses. If you see that you are "running in the red," cut something in order to maintain a balance between income and expense. Disaster awaits you if you continue to operate, say, five percent in the red—in fact, if you continue in the red at all.

Miscellaneous, minor expenses can snowball; these can be difficult to deal with once they get out of hand. It may be necessary to keep a running account of daily expenses for a while in order to get this area under control. Children's allowances must be adjusted for inflation; not adjusting expenses can lead to frustration and arguments in the family. Follow the government's inflation data; it is basically accurate. Credit-buying and borrowing are prime targets for cutbacks: they take money from other categories. Permit no unwise expenditures. Impulse buying can destroy the balance between major expense areas.

On the facing page you will find a budget form to be used in getting (and keeping) mastery over your finances. It incorporates our division of expenses into present necessities, future necessities (savings), and nice but not necessary items. I have filled in some areas under each heading; you should complete the lists in whatever way is appropriate for your situation. The far-left column records normal budget figures. These are the steps for using this form:

1. Determine your income.

2. Determine which expenses fall into the categories of:
   a) necessary expenses,
   b) savings, or
   c) nice but not necessary expenses.

3. List all expenses according to their type.

4. Construct a standard budget in column two, recording standard income and expenditures for each item.

5. Compare totals of income and expenses. Be sure that income is equal to or greater than expenses. If it is not, either add more income or delete some expenses.

6. When you deposit your check, pay the bills listed on your budget as "necessary" before writing any other checks. When they have been paid, circle the amount. If you have

Figure 1: Typical Budget Form

Income/Expenses	Standard Budgeted Amount	Pay Periods												
		1	2	3	4	5	6	7	8	9	10	11	12	13
Income														
Total:														
Expenses														
Necessary:														
Church Support														
Mortgage														
Life Insurance														
Car Payment														
Future Necessities:														
Savings														
Not Necessary:														
Music Lessons														
Nursery School														
Total:														
Income/Expenses:														

missed anything, you will know exactly where to look for it the next pay period.

7. Always record each check you write in your check register.

8. If you write a check to "Cash," make a note of what you intend to spend the cash on, so that you can complete your budget report with that information.

9. Complete your budget report from the information in your check register.

10. Reconcile your bank statement as soon as it comes in. Remember, banks do make mistakes. If you don't know how to do this, get some help.

11. Work at paying off loans and credit-card balances so that you can be free to use the monthly payments for other categories. (One way to work at this is to stop using the credit card until the balance is paid. Then get into the habit of paying the whole bill when due. If you can't pay the whole bill, consider the alternatives to buying.)

As you budget, you will begin to control where your money is spent, and with whom you spend it. Then you will be freer to spend your money on your real needs, to plan ahead and to meet your financial commitments. Sound money-management is more than good record-keeping; it is a key to living responsibly.

CHAPTER ELEVEN

Goals and Actions

MAKING AND KEEPING TO A BUDGET is an essential part of sound money management, but a budget is only a schedule of how you will spend your money during any given pay period. It is not a complete program for managing money. You also need to set realistic goals to indicate in general terms what you want to do with your money. If you don't have goals, there is no reasonable way for you to adjust your budget to new circumstances. Without goals you cannot know why you decided to spend your money the way you did in the past or why you plan to spend it in the way you do in the future.

Any "why" question is a question about goals. Why do I spend my money the way I do? Why do I save a certain portion of my paycheck? Why do I give more to help the poor? Why do I continue to buy things on credit? Such questions help us recognize the guiding principles which lie behind the way we handle our resources.

There are four goals which, I think, have to be part of any worthwhile approach to economic and financial matters. You may add goals to this list, but you should not subtract any.

The first and most basic goal is to use our money to promote the kingdom of God. This goal is essential for any Christian, an automatic part of his economic behavior. Supporting the kingdom means contributing to the Lord's work and giving out of our substance for the relief of the poor. Jesus says that whoever values his life, his possessions, his friends or even his relatives more than he values the Lord is not worthy of the kingdom. Seek first the kingdom in all circumstances.

Second, we should do what is necessary now to maintain our lives under changing economic circumstances. We know that the economy is none too stable. Even if it were in great shape, the wise person knows that it can change suddenly. As provident people we need to be prepared to provide for the necessities of life when the world cannot, or will not, provide them.

The third goal is to live a full human life. We should move our lives in the direction of quality rather than quantity, simplicity rather than complexity, reality rather than illusion, and sobriety rather than flashiness. Beyond this, we know that life is more than just economic survival. God enriches our lives through sports, music, the arts, hobbies and the like. We should receive these with a thankful heart and use some of our resources to enjoy these gifts. Some might consider these simply frills that no one who takes the economic situation seriously should engage in. One can indulge oneself, which is wrong, but to refuse these gifts of God is also wrong. A scene from Corrie ten Boom's *The Hiding Place*, set during World War II, comes to mind. Until they were arrested, the ten Boom family took into their home a number of Jewish refugees. Even in the worst of times they took care to enjoy the things that the Lord had given them.

> And so our "family" was formed. Others stayed with us a day or a week, but these seven remained, the nucleus of our happy household.
>
> That it could have been happy, at such a time and in such circumstances, was largely a tribute to Betsie. Because our guests' physical lives were so very restricted, evenings under Betsie's direction became the door to the wide world. Sometimes we had concerts, with Leendert on the violin, and Thea, a truly accomplished musician, on the piano. Or Betsie would announce "an evening with Vondel" (the Dutch Shakespeare), with each of us

reading a part. One night she talked Eusie into giving Hebrew lessons, another night Meta taught Italian.

The evening's activity had to be kept brief because the city now had electricity only a short while each night, and candles had to be hoarded for emergencies. When the lamps flickered and dimmed we would wind back down to the dining room where my bicycle was set up on its stand. One of us would climb onto it, the others taking chairs, and then while the rider pedaled furiously to make the headlight glow bright, someone would pick up the chapter from the night before. We changed cyclist and reader often as legs or voice grew tired, reading our way through histories, novels, plays (*The Hiding Place*, Fleming H. Revell, 1978, p. 108).

The fourth goal has to do with the conservation of natural resources. God made the resources of the earth to provide for the needs of all mankind. We should be good stewards rather than wasteful consumers.

A goal helps us to set specific courses of action. Analyzing the goal and translating it into practical terms will move us toward the accomplishment of that goal. For example, when I ask what it means for me to put my finances at the disposal of the kingdom, it becomes clear that I need to have a regular pattern of support and contributions. I must give a certain portion of my money to my church. If I belong to a prayer group, fellowship or Christian community, I am obliged to give money to that work also. Scripture also enjoins us to care for the sick, the orphan and the needy, both Christian and non-Christian.

Similarly, in considering the goal of maintaining my life under changing economic circumstances, I must look at the degree to which I am prepared to provide the necessities of life if they become unavailable from outside suppliers.

Food is one essential of life. None of us can depend on an uninterrupted supply of food at the stores. Strikes, blizzards, hurricanes, floods, the high cost of fuel—all might cause an interruption. If inflation outstrips wage increases, it could make food relatively more expensive. We need to be in the position of being able to meet our nutritional needs without depending on outside suppliers. This is, of course, impossible without going full-time into farming and raising livestock, and even then we would depend on outside suppliers for materials to farm and raise animals. A more reasonable approach is to consider storing food. Any stored food is better than none, but a one-month supply is about right. To try to have more on hand would be a heavy financial burden; having much less would not be protection.

Storing food is a classic example of the provident approach to life. Until recently it was common for people to can food and to put fruits and vegetables in root cellars. Although some people continue to do this, the supermarket and the consumer mentality have influenced many of us to live differently. Storing food is not part of some doomsday mentality. Often we hear of it in connection with some imminent "endtime," but if Jesus were coming soon what would we want food for—to bring a picnic lunch to the Supper of the Lamb? Until he comes, it is a mark of a provident and prudent person to have some "food savings" comparable to financial savings.

Water is another necessity of life. The 1993 flooding along the Mississippi River made us all aware of the fragility of the water supply. One filtration plant was knocked out by floodwaters, and the city of Des Moines had to go for weeks on emergency rations. In countries which experience economic hardship, water is rationed regularly. It is turned on only for a couple of hours a day or people must go to a central location and pick it up in containers. If we had a total disaster, the government would probably provide some water for our needs. However, pollution of urban water sources, or the inability of rural wells to function because of electrical outages, is a real possibility. It would make sense to have some kind of water filter in the city and either stored water or the ability to generate electricity in rural areas.

Shelter is another necessity of life. A deteriorating economic situation could affect my ability to keep my home. If I lost my job, or had to take a significant cut in salary, foreclosure on my mortgage would become a real possibility. One option would be to try to pay off the mortgage as soon as possible. To do so would use up most of my money, and I would lose an income deduction at tax time in the bargain. A better way would be to save enough money to continue making the payments. If I never needed to do this, I would still have the money to buy groceries and clothing. A good course of action would be to save something like a year's mortgage payments.

Heat, light, and fuel for cooking food are also necessary elements of life. Fuel for transportation is important. Energy costs are rising and energy is heavily taxed. Much of our energy comes from petroleum and natural gas. The quantities of oil and gas are huge, but they are limited and they are not being replaced, and much of our supply comes from outside the U.S. Wars or terrorism could disrupt the distribution system for oil and gas, rendering them less available and more expensive. It might take several years to work out other distribution systems or to switch over to sources within the U.S.

According to the *World Book Encyclopedia*, the United States consumes about 25 percent of the world's energy, even though it only has about 5 percent of the world's population. A person in a developing country uses only about 6 percent as much energy as a person in one of the developed countries. Europe, Japan and the United States — about 20 percent of the world's population — consume about 70 percent of the world's energy.

Automobiles — which often carry only one person — consume about half the energy used for transportation in the United States. Automobiles are also a major cause of urban air pollution. Efforts at car-pooling and making more fuel-efficient cars have proven only somewhat successful. An affordable, efficient electric car has yet to be produced. Public transportation, on the decline since the 1940s, needs to be brought back and revitalized.

As these facts indicate, provident and resourceful living is not only an ideal, it is rapidly becoming a necessity. Energy is becoming more expensive. Another crisis in the Middle East could result in shortages of gasoline and other petroleum products. The provident and resourceful person must have contingency programs to respond to any sudden interruption in oil imports. Dual fuel capability, adequate standby storage and conservation programs should be high on his priority list.

Electricity can be interrupted by storms. Some utility companies have had temporary power blackouts because of surges in demands. These could get more frequent.

It is a good idea to have an alternate or standby fuel reserve to cover basic needs. Buying new equipment (heaters, lamps, etc.) and large quantities of fuel is expensive. It is also tricky because there are national and local fire codes that govern the storage of fuels. However, if at all possible, it is worth developing the capability to heat and light your house and to cook for a period of two weeks without the use of externally supplied fuels.

Medical care differs from the other necessities. I cannot possibly provide all the medical care that I or my family might need. I cannot, even working with others, have my own hospital, intensive-care ward and surgical teams. In any real emergency, the government would provide major lifesaving medical care, but we should have some first-aid equipment on hand and know how to use it. It would also be wise to have some regularly used medications stored away, on a rotated-use basis.

Cash on hand is also necessary for more things than paying the mortgage or buying groceries. We need to "store" cash in a way that would leave it accessible, not tied up in long-term notes. We should store it where it would not have its value eroded by inflation, as it would if it were kept under the mattress. Savings accounts, bank notes, etc., which yield a good return but which can easily be withdrawn without penalty are smart ways to reserve cash for emergencies. For long-term savings, you might want to look into mutual funds or tax-free trusts.

In times of scarcity, bedding, clothing and shoes might be unavailable or too expensive. Make sure that your family is well provided with these items, and that sewing and repair equipment are available.

Every time I buy gasoline it brings home the importance and expense of transportation in my life. I have already changed my life to adjust to the high cost of gasoline. One summer, we had our family vacation 30 miles from home, not 500 miles away, as we had the previous year. It has made me reflect on the distance between home and work, the fact that we can walk to church and to the store, and that the children could walk to elementary school. I have taken up bicycling. In times of economic uncertainty, the cost and availability of gasoline will continue to be a problem. It is wise now to develop alternatives: bikes, walking and public transportation.

Living a responsible life also means that we need to correct waste and bad planning in our monetary affairs. Budgeting and careful and wise shopping are all important dimensions of wise money management. For most of us, it will mean changing our attitudes and mentality. For some, this will be a wholesale change, for others, a small adjustment. It does little good to store food against possibly difficult times and continue to purchase useless convenience items. It does little good to begin saving money, only to spend it on things we do not need. Developing a provident and resourceful character is the correct overall approach to handling money and possessions well.

The final goal, conserving natural resources, also has a number of important action items built into it. They include: conserving energy and fuels, using recyclable and durable goods, and using products and services that do the least amount of damage to the environment.

These four goals will guide us in our financial planning. In analyzing each goal, we have identified a number of actions which, if implemented, would move us toward a more provident and resourceful life-style, and would protect us against possible economic disorders.

Chapter Twelve

Getting Started

Earlier I listed four responses to the present situation, which I had formulated on the basis of scriptural principles: to develop the character of a provident and resourceful person, to achieve some distance from the world's economic system, to gain effective control over our economic resources, and to plan for the future. The recommendations which followed gave reality to these responses. However, you probably find yourself wondering how in the world you can possibly carry out all the things I have suggested. Most of us are playing catch-up ball; the initial costs will be great. Either this book will go up on the shelf as another interesting book with interesting ideas, or you will accept the general lines of what I propose and begin to make the necessary changes in your life.

It is challenging, but not impossible and certainly not hopeless. There is a way to get started and to carry through on the actions you choose. It lies in planning for the future. The overall approach of this book hinges on good planning. You need to draw up your own plan. Reviewing the elements of such a plan will bring it into focus.

Go back to the scriptural principles and think about your life in the light of them. Ask the Lord to enlighten your mind about how they should be applied in your situation. Ask him, in particular, for honesty in reviewing your life.

Next, look at the goals set forth in the previous chapter. Everything else you do should rest on those goals. As you consider each, ask what you need to do in order to make that goal a reality in your life. The answer will specify the actions you take.

These actions cannot, however, simply be adopted all at once. They must be put in order of priority. In order to determine your priorities, you will have to consider the present state of the economy and what it will probably be like in the next six months. Although we are not economic experts, we do have responsibility to care for ourselves, for those we are responsible for, and for God's work. Begin with an analysis of the present situation. You don't need a Ph.D. in economics to do this. Just read the newspapers and magazines, pay attention to what is going on in your business, your checkbook, your family budget, etc. I am not recommending a detailed study or precise predictions. I am simply suggesting that you develop some feel for what you think will probably happen, and some reasons why you feel the way you do. Then ask yourself whether, on the basis of what you have learned, it is likely that the situation will continue as it has, or get somewhat better or worse in the next six months.

Now ask yourself about events that would have a significant economic impact upon you and their likelihood of occurring in the next six months. A major disaster (tornado, hurricane, earthquake, fire) would have a great impact: even if you yourself were not injured, you would have to depend on others or on government assistance for some basic needs and help in rebuilding. Of course, a major disaster is not very likely, and this will affect the preparations you make, regarding insurance coverage, for example.

On the other hand, in the Great Lakes region of the U.S. where I live, a blizzard or ice storm could easily knock out the electricity for a time, and this could happen in any winter. Hurricanes or tornadoes or earthquakes are more or less likely in different parts of the country. Severe storms are very likely in some locations. Perhaps there will be a large-scale truckers' strike. Perhaps tensions or conflicts in the Middle East may signal a shortage of gasoline. Your six-month look into the future must be continuously updated, and plans must be correspondingly flexible.

Once you have listed some of these likely and not-so-likely events, consider your goals and ask yourself what you would have to do in order to be prepared. When I went through this planning process, I noticed that I depended upon electricity for my water supply (from a well), as well as for lights, heat and refrigeration. I decided that one of my priorities was to buy a portable home generator. If the high cost of heating your home in the winter is going to affect you, consider a woodburning stove. If food shortages are possibilities, grow your own, or can, or store some food. If these somewhat likely events never happen, the steps you have taken will not have harmed you. In fact, approaching life in this way will have the effect of making you a more provident and resourceful person, and this is important no matter what the economic circumstances are.

The principle we all use in taking out liability insurance is helpful. A given event may have a relatively low likelihood of occurring. Yet, if the impact is sufficiently harmful and the cost of the preventative measure is sufficiently low, the preventative measure may reasonably be taken. If the event takes place, responsible planning will have effectively averted panic-stricken responses.

At this point in the process, you should have determined your goals and, with the help of your six-month list of likely events, the actions you will embark upon. The next step is to assign priorities. It will be impossible to do everything at once. The way you order your priorities should be governed by the importance of taking particular actions in the next six months and by the resources you already have on hand. Do not rank them in terms of the amount of money you have to invest; that is a decision that comes later in this process. The order of these items will differ from person to person, but I can give you an example from my own situation. In caring for my family, the most important thing for me was to have some food and water on hand for short-term emergencies and shortages. This meant buying a generator and allocating money to buy food for storage. Second, to cover heating, lighting and cooking, I purchased some kerosene lamps, a kerosene heater and 30 gallons of kerosene.

After you have set some priorities, compare what is needed with what you already possess or have already done. Chances are that you will not start from scratch. You probably already have some food, extra bedding and so on. Now inventory your resources against your needs.

Not every action costs money. Put the actions that do not cost money on a separate list. Begin immediately to implement them in order of their importance.

Other actions do cost money, and most of us do not have much, if any, extra money. How can we possibly implement these actions on limited funds? It can be done. The key is a decision you have already made to sacrifice some things in order to grow in a provident and resourceful way of life. Look at your savings and see what you have. Next, look to your monthly budget and see what can be taken from it. Where can you cut back on expenses to free some money for these actions? Perhaps less money on entertainment or on vacations. Perhaps you could let go of some of your magazine subscriptions. Perhaps you could walk to work, or bike or take public transportation. Each of us can cut back.

Finally, determine how you will allocate the cash you do have. Make a chart like that shown in Figure 2 on the facing page. This will give you a way to make sure that money is allocated for the highest priority item, and also to exercise continuing control. Consider it a supplement to your monthly budget. In fact, have a line in your budget under "necessary items" for those actions each month.

Draw your own chart using Figure 2 as a model, listing the actions in descending order of importance in the far left column. In the far right column, directly across from each action, list the total cost of that action. Between the left- and right-hand columns list the number of months which you are going to take to accomplish these actions: to be realistic you should probably allow 24 to 36 months. Now enter the total amount of money that you can spend per month at the bottom of the month column. Ask yourself how much of that fixed

Figure 2: Budget Supplement Form

Action	Month															Cost of Action
	1	2	3	4	5	6	7	8	9	10	11	12	13	14	15	
Monthly Total:																

amount available to you each month you want to allocate to each action, according to priority.

Figure 3 on the facing page provides an imaginary example to show how this works. On the lowest row is the amount of money available through cutting items judged less important. Suppose that the most important action is to save about $2,500. This money would be used primarily against the possibility of losing a job, or not having enough to pay a mortgage, though it could be used for other emergencies. Second in importance is the acquisition of standby light and heat for the home. Three lamps, a heater and 50 gallons of kerosene would cost $300 in our example. Next, to improve the clothing and bedding situation of the family, it will be necessary to add $25 a month to that part of the regular budget. Storing one month's supply of food will cost $150. These costs are recorded opposite the corresponding action in the right-hand column.

Next, allocate that $225 a month to these actions. Rather than pour all the funds into one action and then into the next, stagger it. This allows progress on a number of actions, thereby increasing the ability to withstand a short-term emergency, which is more likely to happen than a long-term economic disaster. Thus, during the first seven months, money for half the goals will have been set aside. The standby fuel, lamps and heater, the improved clothing and bedding, and the food for storage will have been acquired.

The approach outlined in this chapter will work for you. The entire effort of budgeting, saving, moving away from credit buying, planning and allocating funds will make definite changes in your attitudes, values and character. In fact, one of the best ways to change your character is to do those things that will force change upon yourself.

Figure 3: Budget Supplement Form with Examples

Action	Month 1	2	3	4	5	6	7	8	9	10	11	12	13	14	15	Cost of Action
Increase Savings	$50	$100	$150	$100	$200	$150	$200	$200	$200	$200	$200	$200	$200	$200	$200	$2,550
Emergency Fuel, Lights and Heat	$150	$50	$50	$50												$300
Improve Clothing and Bedding	$25	$25	$25	$25	$25	$25	$25	$25	$25	$25	$25	$25	$25	$25	$25	$375
Store one month Supply of Food		$50		$50		$50										$150
Monthly Total:	$225	$225	$225	$225	$225	$225	$225	$225	$225	$225	$225	$225	$225	$225	$225	

CHAPTER THIRTEEN

Character Formation

MUCH HAS BEEN SAID about implementing actions to achieve some distance from our current economic system, but all these actions are valuable only insofar as they help build our character. Many modern business practices or attitudes toward money and goods tend to undermine rather than to strengthen our character. In fact, we don't hear much about character these days. Most of the ways we are taught to think and talk about people come from modern psychology, which concentrates not on character, but on personality. The goal of clinical psychology is to help people behave more normally or learn to cope with their problems. Most psychological systems are attempts to explain how people came to be troubled and how they might return to normalcy. It is, therefore, only marginally helpful to the healthy.

Character is different from personality. In Greek the word has to do with the engraving and minting of coins, and conveys the idea of marking or stamping. The English word "characteristic" means those things that mark or identify one thing as distinct from another. Character is what makes a person the individual he or she is. Discussing character is something positive, not negative; it has to do with health, not with sickness. It deals with characteristics of a person and asks what these should be. A person of character possesses positive traits.

Scripture presents us with many examples of men and women of character. The woman of Proverbs 31 is presented as a model. She is wise and she teaches others what she knows (v. 26); she is loving, kind and generous (v. 20); she is confident (v. 25); she is dignified (v. 25); she is strong and takes personal initiative (v. 17); she is trustworthy (v. 11); she is provident (vv. 21–22); she is resourceful (v. 27); she is hard-working (vv. 18–19).

Scripture abounds with men of character, too. Job, chapter 29, provides us with a picture of the ideal man, paralleling the Proverbs 31 illustration of the woman of God. This passage portrays a man who takes responsibility for the things which God has put under him. He sat at the "gate of the city" (v. 7), with the rulers and governors, because he ruled over those things he was responsible for; he was a man of wisdom (vv. 9–11); he was a man of justice and mercy (vv. 12–13); he defended the weak and the poor—"I was a father to the needy, and I championed the cause of the stranger. I broke the fangs of the unrighteous, and made them drop their prey from their teeth" (vv. 16–17).

Hebrews, chapter 11, recounts the faithfulness and courage of Abraham, Isaac, Jacob, Joseph, Moses and others— men who were faithful despite great personal suffering and, in some cases, torture and death. The men and women whom the Bible holds up to us are men and women of character. When we compare ourselves to the great men and women of Scripture it is easy to become intimidated. "How could I ever be like them?" Nevertheless, God wants us to be like them and has made it possible.

God made us in his own image: our characters resemble his. Sin has distorted this, but it has not totally nullified it. In sending Jesus, God set about a total restoration of his image in us. He wants us to be marked with his own characteristics, to live his life. He wants us to be able to say with Paul, "The life I live now is not my own; Christ is living in me" (Gal. 2:20 NAB).

God wants us to be perfect, holy and blameless before him, like his Son, who mirrors the glory of the Father.

Be perfect, therefore, as your heavenly Father is perfect (Mt. 5:48).

For this is the will of God, your sanctification. . . . For God did not call us to impurity but in holiness (1 Th. 4:3,7).

Blessed be the God and Father of our Lord Jesus Christ, who has blessed us in Christ with every spiritual blessing in the heavenly places, just as he chose us in Christ before the foundation of the world to be holy and blameless before him in love (Ep. 1:3-4).

Of course, we cannot be perfect and blameless by our own powers. Only God can accomplish this, by living within us. "Those who love me will keep my word, and my Father will love them, and we will come to them and make our home with them" (Jn. 14:23). "Do you not know that you are God's temple and that God's Spirit dwells in you? . . . For God's temple is holy, and you are that temple" (1 Cor. 3:16-17).

The heroes and heroines of Scripture all manifest aspects of God's character. Jesus teaches about those traits, which he forms in those in whom he lives.

Blessed are the poor in spirit, for theirs is the kingdom of heaven.
Blessed are those who mourn, for they will be comforted.
Blessed are the meek, for they will inherit the earth.
Blessed are those who hunger and thirst for righteousness, for they will be satisfied.
Blessed are the merciful, for they will receive mercy.
Blessed are the pure in heart, for they will see God.
Blessed are the peacemakers, for they will be called sons of God.
Blessed are those who are persecuted for righteousness' sake, for theirs is the kingdom of heaven (Mt. 5: 3-10).

These are the characteristics of Jesus himself. He is all these things, and wants us to be like him.

The fruit of the Spirit, described by Paul in Galatians, is also a list of some of the characteristics of God: "love, joy, peace, patience, kindness, generosity, faithfulness, gentleness and self-control" (Gal. 5:22–23). The gifts of the Spirit in Isaiah are prophesied about the Messiah, but they apply prophetically to each of us who lives in Christ: "the spirit of wisdom and understanding, the spirit of counsel and might, the spirit of knowledge and the fear of the Lord" (Is. 11:2).

Becoming men and women of character, then, involves more than some minor changes in our personalities. It means adopting the very characteristics of God's own life as our own. It means allowing God to restore within us the image of his Son.

How is this done? It happens primarily by surrendering our lives more and more to the Lord, so that he can work his changes within us. This is not a matter of being passive. Character is formed by discipline and training. By repeatedly doing the things that we are supposed to do, by adopting and pursuing the actions set forth in this book, we will begin to develop a provident and resourceful character. However, having the character of a provident and resourceful person is only a part of the larger picture. If we pursue the teaching in this book without asking God to form us in the image of his Son, we have missed the point. Preparing ourselves to meet changing economic conditions is not the most important aspect of the life God has called us to. Nor is developing the characteristics of a provident and resourceful person. Important above all else is loving God "with all your heart, and with all your soul, and with all your strength, and with all your mind; and your neighbor as yourself" (Lk. 10:27).

As we attempt to meet the challenges that the modern world sets before us, we should do it in a way that recognizes the Father's love and care for us: "Some are strong in chariots; some, in horses; but we are strong in the name of the Lord, our God" (Ps. 20:8 NAB).

Retirement Planning

PERHAPS THE APPROACHES AND ATTITUDES outlined in this book are unfamilar to you or seem radical or novel. Actually, they may not be so strange at all. You are already familiar with a process which has a lot in common with a provident and resourceful life-style—planning for retirement. A good retirement plan follows many of the basic principles that I am recommending.

Consider the following features of good retirement planning: it takes a long-term view, it makes projections based on the events which are most likely to happen, it involves the accumulation of a variety of skills and assets, it fosters an attitude of self-reliance and openness to change, it is a gradual process which allows you to learn the best strategies as you go along. All this makes perfect sense when thinking about retirement; you will find that it also makes perfect sense when applied in other parts of your life, long before retirement.

This appendix serves two purposes, then. It will help you to clarify the approach that has been described in this book, and it will also present a realistic approach to retirement planning, which is important in itself.

We probably think of retirement as our right, but we would do better to think of it as a gift or an opportunity. It is simply one way, among many, of spending our advancing years, and it is not available to everyone. All around the world, elderly people work until they die or are too feeble to work. They must be cared for by their children and grandchildren. During their lifetimes they can never accrue enough wealth to afford the leisure of retirement.

In most Western countries, however, barring economic catastrophe or the collapse of one's own pension fund, a comfortable, independent retirement will be feasible for those who want it and plan for it.

Old age and retirement are not the same thing. Some people are wealthy enough to retire anytime. In fact, the very rich never need to earn an income in the first place. Many wives are said to "retire" when their husbands do, but they keep working as hard as ever. Some people quit work but end up busier than before, with volunteer projects and hobbies. Old age is a part of life; retirement is a part of your work history.

Because advancing age is simply one segment of life's journey, a provident person will be thinking about it for some time before it happens, making realistic plans. A provident person also prepares for retirement. Retirement requires special preparations, both because it is such a dramatic shift in a person's life-style and because preparations need to be made years and even decades in advance.

There are three areas in which to make preparations for both advancing age and retirement: spiritual, mental and financial.

One basic spiritual principle should be obvious. Even if you choose to retire from your full-time job, you never retire from the Lord's service. He never dispenses you from your obligations to him and to his work. You are still his servant, committed to doing his will and supporting his work with the resources he has granted you. Even after retirement, your first obligation is to God, who gave you life.

Perhaps you are looking forward to retirement with hopes of a spiritual bonanza—finally you will have time to read as much Scripture as you like, to pray regularly, to make the kind of spiritual progress that you have never had the time to make before. Actually, this is unrealistic. The spiritual benefits of retirement will be built upon the foundations you laid previously. A life close to God can be expected to continue into retirement; you can't assume it will begin there.

The coming of retirement also means that you should look at some of your religious beliefs. Work, leisure, rest, service and time are more than practical concerns for a Christian; they have deep theological and spiritual overtones. Your perceptions of the spiritual value of work, of rest, of service, etc., will be important as you face the decision to quit work.

Many Christians view their work as having profound spiritual importance. They understand it as part of God's plan for them; it's much more than simply a way to make money to support themselves and their family. They value their professional labors as a substantial contribution toward the common good or to the betterment of their fellow human beings.

Some Christians view leisure as akin to laziness or idleness. They will recall Paul's admonition, "Anyone unwilling to work should not eat. For we hear that some of you are living in idleness, mere busybodies, not doing any work" (2 Th. 3:10-11). Does your understanding of Scripture convince you that God provides no resting place for us here on earth, that we should expect to rest only in heaven?

How do you, as a Christian, understand the relationship between work and leisure? Does your commitment to a life of service to God and others allow you a period at the end of your life when you take it easy, relax, sit comfortably in the shade? For some believers, the very notion of stopping work may strike them as shameful: "Do I have the right to take it easy when I can still be of some use?"

In all these questions, it is important to be aware of your personal beliefs and standards, in light of how you have heard God's word addressed to you, both through your church and through your perception of God's plan for your life. In retiring, as in everything else, it is essential that you set your decisions in the context of God's will for you.

There is no law requiring you to cease all activity after retirement. Perhaps your level of energy will allow you to take on even more responsibilities; perhaps not. Perhaps you will fill your time with other money-making activities; perhaps not. Perhaps you will sit tight and enjoy a well-earned rest; perhaps not. In all things, God's intentions for you are the only sure guidance.

"Tell the older men to be temperate, serious, prudent, and sound in faith, in love, and in endurance. Likewise, tell the older women to be reverent in behavior, not to be slanderers or slaves to drink; they are to teach what is good. . . . " (Ti. 2:2–3). Old age should bring a measure of spiritual maturity, and spiritually mature people have many gifts to share with younger members of the body of Christ. The long-term vantage of advancing age brings wisdom and insight into the mysteries of life and of God's will. The suffering that a person has endured over the years can evoke compassion and words of wisdom for those who are enduring their own portion of suffering now. A lifetime of faithfulness to God is itself a striking lesson to the young, who see that perseverance brings victory over temptations and discouragement.

"You have received without paying, so give without being paid" (Mt. 10:8 TEV). The wisdom of the elderly is a precious resource for the young. The elderly should be open-handed and generous in passing on what they have learned from God through the years.

The second area where you need to prepare well for retirement and old age is mental or attitudinal. You need a clear understanding of what you will be getting into; otherwise your preparations will not be realistic. If you look forward to retirement with the wrong assumptions or expectations, your preparations will be inadequate.

Sometimes people look forward to someone else's retirement, someone they have known in the past. They assume that they will have Uncle Joe's health problems or Dad's bitterness or Cousin Martha's continual lack of money. These emotional attitudes can color one's preparations, so dispose of them as soon as you can identify them. You are preparing for your own future, and a great part of it is under your control.

What are the right attitudes to have? First, of course, is the stinging realization: I will someday be feeble. I will someday not be as strong, healthy, mentally quick or eager to work as

I am now. Yet, there is another related insight: I will someday be a lot more experienced, self-controlled and insightful than I am now. Old age brings its blessings as well as its curses. The ripening of a personality means that lessons have been learned, that you will not make nearly as many mistakes as you did when you were young. You will understand more about life. You will be more secure when you face decisions.

You will also understand yourself better. You'll know better what your real needs are, what is important to you, what makes you happy and contented and what makes you angry and miserable. You will be more realistic about what you expect from yourself and from others.

So, if you plan for the worst you are probably being too pessimistic, and if you plan for the best you are probably being too optimistic. The key is to be realistic, after looking at your unique situation and your prospects. The future decades are largely unknown, but it is important to plan for them rationally rather than emotionally.

As retirement looms in your planning, reassess your attitudes about elderly people in general, about your ability to change, about what your real needs will be. If the Lord is your rock, you will realize that this is just one more stage among the many he has already guided you through. With faith in him, you have made adjustments before, and you can make them again. His plan for you continues intact through retirement and beyond.

In our society, the gradual process of growing older is punctuated by the singular event of retirement. It is a watershed between two very different styles of life. Besides the major change from working full-time to not working full-time, retirement also means a sudden decrease in income, an increase in personal time, and perhaps also a complete geographical change of home, friends and acquaintances, along with changed relationships with family members. While most retirees don't move to a condo in Florida, the change in lifestyle can still be quite dramatic.

Mental preparation for such a dramatic shift is essential, especially since we tend to get set in our ways as the years go by. In fact, mental preparation is much more important than financial preparation. You can be happy without a lot of money, but you won't be happy if you are permanently disrupted by retirement. For example, if you have spent 40 or more working years feeling useful, appreciated and indispensable at your job, then you may be in for quite a shock when it turns out you were not so indispensable after all. "The company seems to get along fine without me." Or, if you have always valued your ability to help others, you may be disappointed and distraught when people make fewer and fewer requests of you, in deference to your age. "Nobody seems to need my help anymore." Attitudes like these can sour your life, even in that expensive condo in Florida.

One good piece of advice: plan for an active retirement. Most Americans won't be worn out physically by their jobs. In fact, they will probably have more health problems related to life-style—smoking, lack of exercise, overeating, anxiety— than to their job environment. Plan to keep actively involved in life, even if you know you'll have to slow down somewhat.

With the pressure off and a free schedule, you'll have opportunities to do many things you could only do occasionally when you were working full-time: golf, art, cooking, visiting the kids and grandkids, social work, going back to school, reading, teaching, volunteer church work, travel, entertaining friends, preparing for Christmas, refinishing furniture, writing, exercise, hobbies, just plain relaxing.

One fellow I know approached retirement age telling his fellow workers, "There are things I've been wanting to do for years, and now I'll finally have time to do them." As it turned out, though, the "things" he had planned for years amounted to only one—cleaning out the garage. He accomplished that during the first week after retirement and then started sitting around the house watching TV and getting on his wife's nerves.

Plan for a full life after retirement. Something may intervene to prevent this, but it is still far better than making no plans or planning to do nothing.

Here is where your character formation as a provident and resourceful person becomes all-important. Much of our retirement planning—especially in the years from our 20s to our 40s—is necessarily imprecise and generalized. However, we can still be building the kind of good character traits which will be helpful when we grow old. Self-reliance, practical knowledge, skills, talents—these are assets throughout life, including old age. Even before we can get very specific about our plans, we can be building the character traits we will need in the future.

For example, are you a self-starter? Left to your own devices, will you take charge of the time available or will you sit around and do nothing? This trait will be helpful when you don't have a 40-hour-per-week job organizing your time for you. Can you set goals and meet them? Can you plan realistically for the future? Do you give up more often than you persevere?

Begin now to develop the kind of character which will adapt well to retirement. Imagine what your life-style will look like then. Consider what you would like to be doing, the kind of activities you want to do. Most often, there will not be a radical shift: you will simply have more time to do the things you have already been doing on the side. Before retiring you could only visit the kids once a year; then you will be able to visit them twice or three times a year, and do some other traveling. Hours spent at a hobby can increase; you can take more time preparing for holidays instead of fitting preparations in around your job commitment. In fact, in the years immediately before retirement, you could decide to start spending more time on the activities you will want to pursue in earnest after you retire. It's much better to increase your time on a hobby than to try and start it outright the week after retirement. Don't tell yourself you'll take up dog-breeding after you retire when you've never even had a pet terrier. It probably won't work. The impact of this major shift into retirement can be eased if you begin some of your retirement activities before you stop working.

At first glance, financial preparations for advancing age and retirement might seem to be the simplest of all: save money. Build up a nest egg. Start saving for that rainy day. However, the way you save money is just as important as the amount you save.

First, start early. You should begin saving for retirement as soon as you start bringing in a regular salary. Make it part of your monthly budget. This advice might seem impractical for a young couple trying to keep the kids in shoes and clothing, not to mention college, but it makes sense. The reason is a simple one—compound interest (or reinvesting dividends). One of my accountant friends has called compound interest the "eighth wonder of the world." One current television commercial gives this example. Start saving $300 a month when you're 23 and you will retire a millionaire; wait until you're 30 to start and you'll retire with $600,000; wait until age 40 and you'll finish with $200,000. The earliest money you put into interest-bearing accounts will make the most money for you.

Second, save regularly. Set up a schedule and keep to it, barring emergencies or disasters. Retirement is a sure thing; you will need the money. You are not saving for a house fire or major illness—events which might or might not happen. You are saving for retirement, which will happen.

Third, set financial goals, making them more specific as time goes on. Decide on the kind of life you want to live after retirement. If you opt for the Florida condo, start planning how you will pay for it. One alternative is to start looking for a good buy when you're in your 50s. If you find one, you can purchase it, use it for vacations and lease it out until you're ready to move in yourself. You might even make some profit in the meantime. The same goes for any major purchases you will make after retiring: a boat, cottage on the lake, membership in a golf club, sports equipment, mobile home or RV. Purchasing such major items while you are still earning a salary makes a lot of sense.

Refine your goals as retirement age approaches. When you're 30, under pressure from a career-building job, you may look forward to a retirement of mint juleps on the front porch swing, doing nothing. By the age of 55, however, you might look forward to visiting the grandkids all across the country or joining the Peace Corps. The 10 years before retirement are the time to start getting specific; before then, just save money.

Money, of course, is a complicated subject, since it gains and loses its value over time. Inflation, purchasing power and the increasing interdependence of all currencies affect the value of your money. Many people prefer to seek what they call "financial security," which is different from simply piling up money. This involves a wide variety of investments, hedges against inflation, real assets, etc. No matter which course you choose, the key thing is to start preparing early.

Your options range from simple savings accounts (not a very good option at present) to varieties of tax-deferred annuities (pretty good), individual retirement accounts (also good), pension funds, investments (stocks, artwork) and the accumulation of assets (house, business, jewelry, land, etc.). You may feel fine about subjecting some of your extra money to the high risk of grain futures, for example, but don't use your retirement funds for that. You *will* need this money later.

An ideal arrangement is to set aside enough money to generate a retirement income for yourself: each month you live on the proceeds from your investments. You never need to dip into the principal. This may be beyond the reach of most retirees, but it might be something to shoot for.

The Social Security Administration will provide a measure of assistance to you in your old age, but many planners nowadays estimate that such funds will amount to only one-fourth of what a middle-aged person today will feel comfortable living on in retirement. More important will be the medical insurance which comes through Medicare and Medicaid. Currently, health insurance is under review in the U.S., so future programs may be quite different from current programs. It does look as if the government will continue to be involved with health insurance for the elderly for the foreseeable future, but it is difficult to predict what it will look like for others, even over the next 10 years.

The best plan is to see government programs as helpful assistance, but not the major source of your income.

It is also important, as far as you are able, to diversify your financial preparations for retirement. Strategies which are good under today's conditions should change as the years go by. In the early 1990s, interest rates fell, inflation decreased and the rates of return on CDs, bonds and mutual funds all changed. As rates lowered in one area and rose in others, many investors shifted their money around to earn greater income. Many millions of dollars went from CD investments into mutual funds, for example, with a little increase in risk but much better profit than the CDs could offer at the time.

In the future, interest rates may rise dramatically again and those same amounts of money could flow back into CDs out of mutual funds. Some people decided to keep their money in the CDs and insured bonds, because they wouldn't allow any of their retirement funds to go into risky areas. U.S. Savings Bonds and other insured or government-backed bonds do not pay the best interest, but they are safer than other investments. If you want your retirement money to be as safe as humanly possible, you will have to select your investments carefully. A lot depends on your tolerance for risk and your peace of mind. However, you should always keep retirement money in relatively low-risk options.

It's good not to pay too much attention to this kind of long-term, regular savings plan. If you keep weekly track of your mutual fund's earnings (or lack of them), you will be tempted to make too many administrative changes, which often cost you money. Every so often, take a look at the rate of profit, relative to other options. If you make a change, do so cautiously.

Do not let yourself be talked into a get-rich-quick scheme with your retirement funds. Risk other money, if you feel you have to, but keep your retirement money intact. Add to it regularly, and perhaps in a way that doesn't attract your attention, such as payroll deduction. If your company offers a secure payroll-deduction plan for retirement, contribute the maximum amount allowable (particularly if the amount is tax-deferred).

Though there are exceptions, the overall trend in this country is definitely up for retirees. People are now talking about something like a national retirement plan, and such things as pension portability are favored by many legislators.

This trend may change, but currently it looks as if retirement is becoming easier and more comfortable for most Americans. I don't think you should bank on this for the long-term future, though. The Social Security program could change; isolated pension funds have failed in the past and will fail in the future. Make your own plans, so that you will be able to maintain your independence and life-style according to your own intentions.

In considering your assets for retirement, pay particular attention to your home. If you own your home outright, it may be possible to sell it or remortgage it. This will generate a large sum of money to begin retirement with. You could invest this money or use it for some major outlay: a recreational vehicle, a lakeside cabin in Minnesota, a small farm with an apple orchard, the franchise for a small business.

Understandably, many people look at their home as essential to their future security: "At least I'll still have my home; they can't take that away." This kind of reasoning may or may not be realistic. To take an extreme example, would you decide to scrimp on food so you could continue living in your $250,000 house, or could you downsize to a $90,000 house with a 40-year mortgage? Then you could make your monthly mortgage payments out of the proceeds and get some usefulness out of the money that's tied up in your house. (Recall, the IRS allows you, once in a lifetime, to take the profit from the sale of your home as untaxed income.)

Perhaps your home is still just right for your needs. It might be feasible to raise some cash by remortgaging it, or arranging what is called a reverse mortgage. When you retire, there may be other options available. That's the time to make specific plans. The key is to remain flexible and open.

A provident person is always investigating, reading, considering and asking "What if?" questions. Listen to reputable advisors on retirement planning and investing. Think carefully about your major decisions. Be realistic. Especially, keep your family and friends in mind. Family and friends will make retirement more enjoyable—much more so than having a posh life on a Caribbean island where you don't know anyone.

If, over the course of your life, you follow the general

principles of this book, you will have won a great deal of practical knowledge and experience by the time you retire from full-time work. You will understand that everything changes over time, and you will have experience at being flexible in the face of change. You will also know what your talents and skills are, and how they can be put to use. Some of your skills will probably be marketable after you retire. Your knowledge of how to fix small appliances, for example, could set you up in a part-time money-making job. Home-canned specialty jellies could also be a popular item at craft fairs. There is no law against continuing to make money after you retire (though this might affect the amount you receive from Social Security).

There is a reversal which occurs after retiring. Instead of saving money up in your nest egg, you start spending money out of your nest egg. This can be a frightening prospect, as you see your bank balance decreasing with no realistic way to increase it again. Yet, this was what you were saving the money for in the first place. Again, this is where years of resourceful living will be your biggest asset. You will feel confident in your ability to do well under whatever conditions you find yourself. Even if you haven't been able to meet the goals you set for retirement savings, and your nest egg only amounts to a few thousand dollars, your character will be such that you will meet this challenge directly and make the best of the situation.

Most likely, your planning and preparation will bear the fruit of peace, strength and wisdom as you enjoy your advancing years.

Resources

At the public library, check these headings in the subject card catalog for books and the periodical index for magazine articles.

Automobiles
Clothing
Consumer education
Consumer protection
Cost and standard of living
Credit
Debt
Economics
Employment
Finance, personal
Food
Food preservation
Food storage
Health
Health information services
House
House buying
Insurance
Investments
Money
Pensions
Retirement
Saving
Taxation
Thrift

Water
Water purification

You may have some of these magazines in your library:

American Health
Consumer Reports
Consumer's Digest
Consumer's Research
Forbes
Fortune
Kiplinger's Personal Finance Magazine
Money

Other magazines where you might find useful articles:

Back Home
P.O. Box 370
Mountain Home, NC 28758

Harrowsmith Country Life
Ferry Road
Charlotte, VT 05445

Mother Earth News
P.O. Box 56304
Boulder, CO 80323–6304

Some of the many books available:

Yvonne G. Baker, *Guilt-Free Cooking* (Accent Books)
Mary Carse, *Wilderness Cook Book* (P.O. Box 625, Shelburne, VT 05482)
Deaf Smith Country Cookbook (Avery)
Barbara Densley, *The A B C's of Home Dehydration* (Horizon)
H. Bud Franklin, *The Squawk Book* (Webejamn)
Matthew Lesko and Andrew Naprawa, *The Great American Gripe Book: Over 1000 Government Offices You Can Contact to Complain, Right a Wrong, Get Satisfaction* (Information USA, Inc., Kensington, MD)

Doris Janzen Longacre, *Living More With Less* (Herald Press) and *More With Less Cookbook* (Herald Press)

Malcolm MacGregor, *Financial Planning Guide for Your Money Matters* (Bethany House)

Malcolm MacGregor and Stanley C. Baldwin, *Your Money Matters* (Bethany House)

Ralph Nader and Clarence Ditlow and the Center for Auto Safety, *The Lemon Book* (Moyer Bell)

Ralph Nader and Wesley J. Smith, *The Frugal Shopper* (Public Citizen Health Research Group, Washington, DC, 202/833–3000)

Ralph Nader and Wesley J. Smith, *Winning the Insurance Game* (Knightsbridge)

Reader's Digest Consumer Adviser: An Action Guide to Your Rights

Reader's Digest Household Hints and Handy Tips

Virginia Schomp, *Better Business Bureau A to Z Buying Guide* (Holt)

Chris Harold Stevenson, *Auto Repair Shams and Scams* (Price Stern Sloan)

Free and low-cost federal publications:

Consumer Information Catalog
Box 100
Pueblo, CO 81002

Helpful consumer publications:
(Monthly magazine and annual buying guide)

Consumer Reports
Box 51166
Boulder, CO 80321–1166

(Selection of consumer-oriented books)

The Consumer Reports Money Book
Homeowner's Legal Guide
How To Buy a House, Condo, or Co-op
How To Sell a House, Condo, or Co-op

How To Plan for a Secure Retirement
Mayo Clinic Family Health Book
Money Management Basics

Write: Consumer Reports Books
      9180 LeSaint Drive
      Fairfield, OH 45014–5452

Basic products:

Martens Health and Survival Products, Inc.
5365 Avenida Encinas #F
Box 725
Carlsbad, CA 92008
800/824–7861 (USA), 800/822–5984 (CA), 619/438–0866

More books from Greenlawn Press to strengthen you in your Christian walk!

Fathers, Come Home:
A Wake-Up Call for Busy Dads
By Bill Swindell

National family advocate Bill Swindell offers sound father-to-father advice on why we must abandon life in our self-absorbed worlds and begin active parenting. Our kids need—and deserve—nothing less! This book, filled with touching stories and hard-earned wisdom, will be a help to any dad striving to be the father God wants him to be.

$7.95, paper, 101 pp.

Home Child Care:
The Tender Business
By Ellie Roosli Peters

With years of experience, a solid business sense and, most importantly, strong Christian convictions about the ministry of caring for children, Ellie Peters shares her insights about this "tender business." Mrs. Peters gives thorough and useful information on home safety, recreational and educational activities, nutrition, children's growth and development, discipline and basic business practices.

$5.95, paper, 97 pp.

God Is at Work in You:
A Practical Guide to Growth in the Spirit
By Ralph Rath

God Is at Work in You is perfect for anyone who has just come to know the Lord. Yet it also refreshes and inspires any Christian wanting to grow in zeal for the Lord. Each chapter includes Scripture readings, real-life examples and discussion questions. Topics include praying daily, overcoming sin, discerning God's will and sharing the gospel with others.
"Would you like your Christian life to soar with the Spirit? Here's a book that will show you how."

—Bert Ghezzi, former editor, *Charisma*
$5.95, paper, 92 pp.

Seven Steps Toward God
By Bill Beatty

Filled with practical wisdom, *Seven Steps Toward God* gives clear steps for accepting God's love and lordship and for living according to his plan. Beatty, an internationally known speaker and evangelist, helps readers pattern their lives after Jesus. He includes Scripture passages for reflection, making his book ideal for group instruction and retreats or for personal use.

$4.50, paper, 102 pp.

To Serve As Jesus Served
By Clem Walters

Ideal for small groups and adult-education programs, *To Serve As Jesus Served* is also suitable for personal use. This very popular book helps Christians serve with less frustration and more joy. Talk outlines, discussion questions and suggestions for practical application are included. The course was used and tested for more than 10 years before publication in book form, benefitting thousands. Now in its fourth printing!

$5.95, paper, 132 pp.

Order these books today from your local Christian bookstore or directly from:
Greenlawn Press
Dept. K1
107 S. Greenlawn Ave.
South Bend, IN 46617

Payment must accompany order. Please add 7% for shipping and handling (**$2.00 minimum**). Payment may be by check, money order, Visa or Mastercard. If paying by credit card, please include your credit card number, your name as it appears on the card, the expiration date of your card, your phone number, and your signature on your order.

You can also order by phone using your Visa or Mastercard. Phone us at 219-234-5088 (no collect calls) or fax 219-236-6633 between 8:30 AM and 4:30 PM EST, Monday through Friday. Please have your credit card ready when you call.